# WORK AND EMPLOYMENT IN LIBERAL DEMOCRATIC SOCIETIES

# *Liberal Democratic Societies*

SERIES EDITORS: ROGER MICHENER AND EDWARD SHILS

## Civility and Citizenship
EDWARD BANFIELD

## Morality and Religion
GORDON L. ANDERSON AND MORTON A. KAPLAN

## The Mass Media
STANLEY ROTHMAN

## Nationality, Patriotism and Nationalism
ROGER MICHENER

## Work and Employment
DAVID MARSLAND

## Democracy in Non-Western States
DENNIS AUSTIN

## The Balance of Freedom:
## Economy, Law, and Learning
ROGER MICHENER

Liberal Democratic Societies is part of a larger series on World Social Systems by Morton A. Kaplan, General Editor. The other systems examined are the Soviet System, series editor Alexander Shtromas, and China, series editor Ilpyong J. Kim. These books are available from:

 ## *PWPA Books*
2700 University Avenue West, Suite 47
St. Paul, MN 55114, USA
Phone (612) 644-2809 ☐ Fax: (612) 644-0997

# WORK AND EMPLOYMENT IN LIBERAL DEMOCRATIC SOCIETIES

*Edited by*

David Marsland

*Paragon House*

*A PWPA Book*
*St. Paul, Minnesota*

Published in the United States of America by
Professors World Peace Academy
2700 University Avenue West
St. Paul, Minnesota 55114

*A Professors World Peace Academy Book*

The Professors World Peace Academy (PWPA) is an international
association of professors and scholars from diverse backgrounds,
devoted to issues concerning world peace. PWPA sustains a program
of conferences and publications on topics in peace studies, area and
cultural studies, national and international development, education,
economics and international relations.

Library of Congress Catalog-in-Publication Data

Work and employment in liberal democratic societies / edited by
David Marsland.
      p. cm. — (Liberal democratic societies)
"A PWPA book."
Includes bibliographical references.
ISBN 0-943852-67-6. — ISBN 0-943852-68-4 (pbk.)
    1. Quality of work life. 2. Democracy. 3. Work—Social aspects.
4. Work ethic. I. Marsland, David, 1939- . II. Series: World social
systems. Liberal democratic societies.
HD4904.W643 1994
306.3"6—dc20                             93-46969
                                             CIP

# TABLE OF CONTENTS

# SERIES EDITORS' FOREWORD

Liberal democratic societies, as patterns of political, economic and social arrangements, would seem to be vindicated against their detractors. Until recently Marxism in its various forms and other proponents of single party states and centrally planned economies appeared to offer realistic and allegedly beneficial alternatives to liberal democracy. Events in China, the Soviet Union, Eastern Europe, and the Third World have so reduced the persuasiveness of these arguments that there are no readily apparent alternatives to liberal democratic societies.

Nevertheless, the discomfitures and embarrassments of single party states should not be regarded as a justification for complacency. We should be appreciative of the merits of liberal democratic societies, but we should be aware of their shortcomings, in light of their own ideals, and of the dangers to which they are liable.

The purpose of the present series of books is to take stock of and to assess, in a historical perspective, the most central achievements and shortcomings of liberal democratic societies, and to encourage thought on their maintenance and improvement.

Not only do we seek to delineate some of these main lines of historical development of the variant forms of liberal democracy, but we also seek to discern certain fundamental postulates that are common to these institutions and processes. In this way, we hope to define more clearly the liberal democratic ideal and its limits. We wish to learn where the practice falls short of the ideal or deforms it. We wish to form an estimate of the destructive forces within the liberal democratic ideal itself and of their potentialities for causing its deteriorization or its collapse. We wish above all to learn how these destructive potentialities may be averted.

This series insists on the bond between liberalism and

democracy. Liberalism and democracy are two distinguishable components of present-day liberal democratic societies. Their combination into a particular form of society is a great achievement but it is also a source of difficult problems. For instance, can these societies reconcile the fundamental conflict between minimizing governmental authority and intrusiveness and the democratic demand for more governmental activities and greater governmental provision of welfare services? What are the consequences of some of the institutions of liberal democratic society for the daily life of the individual in his or her private sphere? These questions and others like them constitute a continuing challenge for the present and successor generations. These books are devised to assist in the understanding of that challenge.

*Roger Michener*
*Edward Shils*

# INTRODUCTION

*David Marsland*

Work remains today, as ever, a fundamental element of social life, and central to human concerns. As far as liberal democratic societies specifically are concerned, there are few factors as crucial to their future prospects as work—in particular the values of the work ethic, the efficiency and equity of recruitment to work roles, the nature of rewards for work, and the relations between the state and employing organizations.

It can sometimes seem, if we were to judge from the contemporary images constructed by the media and by the arts, that liberal democratic societies are mere playgrounds of leisure and arenas of self-indulgent hedonism. Neither journalists and social scientists nor novelists, film directors and television program-makers emphasize often or positively the regular, disciplined, exerted, rewarding endeavor entailed in all work.

Yet it is in liberal democratic societies, above all others, that work has become and remains fundamental and central to the culture as a whole. Indeed, "industrial societies" so-called might better be labeled "work societies." This collection brings together expert analyses of why work is so important in free societies, how work has to be organized if such societies are to stay free, and the dangers posed for freedom and democracy by attitudes and institutions which misconstrue and impede individual work effort.

In Chapter 1, Professor Al Himelson, an American sociologist, sets the scene for the whole book by examining the established role of work as a key mechanism of social solidarity in modern societies. He explores the threats to that role posed by a range of contemporary developments including in particular technological innovation, weakening of family and locality, and distortions in welfare provision.

In Chapter 2, John Chodes, a nineteenth-century specialist, provides a historical underpinning for the analysis of work in contemporary society. He shows graphically how reactionary forces–including British aristocrats and German socialists–sought from an early stage in the process of industrialization to control and subjugate free labor.

In Chapter 3, David Marsland, a sociologist and social policy analyst, offers a critical examination of the dangerously negative attitudes toward work evinced by most modern social scientists. Contrasting this with the strongly positive attitudes of the general population, he argues that a positive work culture is essential if economic prosperity and political freedom are to be maintained.

In Chapter 4, Professor Peter Saunders, a dissident among contemporary British sociologists in his persistent refusal to do other than call a factual spade a spade, focuses in detail on one important aspect of the distortions criticized by Marsland. He demonstrates, on the basis of up-to-date empirical evidence, that—far from being rigid and class-ridden—contemporary Britain is, like other liberal democratic societies, characterized by high rates of occupational and social mobility, and meritocratic to a remarkable degree.

The following two chapters focus sharply on the primary threat to autonomous work and rational labor markets—the welfare system. In Chapter 5, Professor Ralph Segalman, a well-known investigator of poverty in America, examines the creation over recent decades of a helpless, dependent underclass resulting from mistakes in the nature and extent of welfare provision. He argues that the underclass comprises s dangerous impediment to the operation of an efficient economy, and in the long run, a serious threat to freedom.

In Chapter 6, Professor Theo Roy, a distinguished political scientist from New Zealand, broadens Segalman's critique with a powerful demonstration of the destructive effects of welfare not only on work practices and performance, but also and beyond that on the whole character of the free and responsible individual.

In the two subsequent chapters, the special situations of two key subgroups—ethnic minorities and young people—vis-à-vis work and the economy are examined respectively by Professor Walter Williams, the distinguished American economist (Chapter 7), and by Dr. Adrian Furnham, a British psychologist responsible for some of the most interesting recent empirical investigations of real world social behavior (Chapter 8). In both cases, the authors argue, the situations and needs of minorities merit careful attention if serious problems for the world of work as a whole are to be avoided.

The collection concludes with a pair of chapters which examine, in turn, the persisting constants and the unpredictably impending future of work in free societies. In Chapter 9, Dr. Dennis O'Keeffe analyses the role of work as an arena for the formation and utilization of individual and collective human capital. In Chapter 10, a respected Italian social scientist, Professor Tamborlini, provides a careful examination of likely trends in the development of work in coming decades.

Chapters 3, 4, 5, 9, and 10 are based on papers presented to a Professors World Peace Academy Conference in London on liberal democracy. The other chapters were specially commissioned by the editor.

## WORK AND EMPLOYMENT

There were many distinct causes of the failure and collapse of socialism which was symbolized by the fall of the Berlin Wall. Not the least significant among them was a doctrinaire misconstrual of the real nature of work which is inherent in socialist ideology.

Socialists are correct in their emphasis on the importance of work, and hence in their principled antipathy to unemployment. They are gravely mistaken, however, in their interpretation of the meaning of the importance of work, and hence in their prescriptions for a cure for unemployment.

Work is not essentially, or indeed even primarily, a merely instrumental means to material livelihood. Nor, therefore, can it be properly encompassed within the trite slogan of the right to employment, or engineered into existence by the state apparatus. Work is rather man's normal and natural mode and arena of individual creativity, self-expression, and competitive achievement. Within free societies, this arena is liberated from arbitrary authoritarian interference, and the human scope for creativity, self-expression, and achievement is thus maximized. Free labor and freedom as such are psychologically and institutionally inseparable.

Work is also and equally, besides its constitutive role in the character of free individual persons, a fundamental characteristic of the free society and of liberal culture. Wherever work is misunderstood and mishandled, wherever it is treated merely as a welfare right or as a civic duty, we can be sure that slavery, in one form or another, is either already established or imminently impending.

If work—properly understood and appropriately organized—is thus fundamental to basic human aspirations and to the essentials of human nature, and if it is also constitutive of the ultimate structure of the free society, then the cost of interfering with natural and normal work systems is bound to be high indeed. Little wonder if socialism fails and is doomed to fail wherever men yield to its temptations.

- If the state appropriates the rights and responsibilities of entrepreneurs, new and genuine work cannot be created.
- If the state seizes for itself the right to employ workers, genuine employment is squeezed out of existence.
- If the state presumes to plan the productive system and the labor market, the normal and natural mechanisms which create and maintain real work—property, the family, an independent legal system, and the market—wither and die.
- If the state seeks to equalize and otherwise to manipulate work incentives, motivation dries up, and only force is left as a mechanism for securing compliance with a prosperous society's work requirements.
- If the state prevents individuals from seeking and retaining just rewards for their work on behalf of themselves as individuals and their families, people's natural initiative and enterprising effort are either stifled or distracted into destructive activities.
- If the state seeks to reduce unemployment by inventing specious work or by paying the workforce on anything but a temporary and modest basis for doing nothing or next to nothing, society's resources are squandered, and the whole basis of the work ethic is sabotaged.

All of this is what has happened—and not accidentally, but as a result of deliberate ideological intent—under socialism. Hence, in large part, its disastrous and inevitable failure, and the collapse of socialist societies into economic bankruptcy, moral vacuity, and civil strife.

If these destructive outcomes are to be avoided in the free world, we shall have to learn the hard lessons of failed socialism, and handle work wisely and well. We must at all costs, and despite whatever seductive temptations, preserve and strengthen the cultural values and the institutional arrangements which are essential to a free labor market and a liberal economy.

## WORK AND EMPLOYMENT

In Europe there are currently powerful forces at work pressing the peoples of the continent in the dangerously destructive directions mapped out by socialists. The Social Charter of the European Community and the so-called "Social Chapter" of the Maastricht Treaty would rapidly hedge the work system about with controls and regulations which would destroy it within decades. In the United States and in the rest of the free world, except perhaps Japan, hysterical reactions to high levels of unemployment threaten a similar outcome over a longer period.

All such pressures must be resisted vigorously. Only by preservation of the work ethic, a free labor market, and a liberal economy can we bring unemployment down to tolerable levels, and only thus can we secure for the people of our democratic nations the freedom which is indeed their genuine right.

# CHAPTER 1

# WORK AND SOCIAL SOLIDARITY

*Alfred Himelson*

The nature and organization of work continues to undergo profound changes, as it has almost continuously since the beginning of the industrial revolution. The nineteenth century and the first three-quarters of the twentieth century were characterized by the preeminence of the large industrial plant utilizing mass production techniques, the appearance of the professional manager, and the legitimation of the mass labor union. In the last quarter of this century the nature of work and work organization is once again shifting. It is being driven by changes in technology and changes in society which will probably result in a lesser degree of social solidarity in the workplace. Before discussing the changes themselves, it is necessary to examine the social and economic environment in which they are taking place.

## SOCIAL SOLIDARITY

In the second half of the twentieth century we are witnessing an acceleration of the rate at which traditional forms of social solidarity are breaking down or weakening. The reasons for these changes are quite different from the factors often linked to the transformations of these institutions in earlier periods: war, pestilence, economic or natural disaster. While the breakdown of solidarity is from many factors, the influence of three forces are especially noteworthy.

The first is the increasing dominance of an extreme variety of individualism that stresses personal happiness unfettered by responsibility to others. Tocqueville defined this as 'egoism', which he said is a "...passionate and exaggerated love of self which leads a man to think of all things in terms of himself and to prefer himself to all" (Tocqueville 1969, 506-507). It is at the opposite end of the social continuum from sentiments of 'solidarity' which stem from a sense of being joined with others because of common responsibilities or interests. At one time, behavior resulting from egoistic attitudes was seen as selfish and therefore socially disapproved. At the present time, there is increasing legitimation for such actions.

The second factor weakening social solidarity is the growth of feelings of 'disenchantment' among the populations of modernized countries. This has happened because there has been a loss of faith in the sacred and in those norms that had acquired a connection with the sacred. What substituted for the sacred was a belief in a rationality that stressed technological discovery, utilitarianism and efficiency as means of achieving the goals of the 'good society'.

There has also, however, been a second disenchantment, whose nature has not been so clearly recognized. This has to do with the introduction of powerful new forms of knowledge. The use of research and evaluation methods have shown that many programs and projects that were assumed to be successful were, when subjected to examination by these techniques, found to be of no substantial value, or in some cases quite worthless. This has led to strong feelings of disenchantment and alienation on the part of large segments of the populace, who feel they have been betrayed by uncaring or incompetent officials. This in turn has led to the withdrawal of many people from the area of public affairs and heightened their cynicism about the worth of most large-scale institutions. The reality is that the officials and politicians of the present era are probably no more uncaring or incompetent than were their counterparts of bygone years. We just know more today about what they are able to accomplish or not accomplish.

The third factor is associated with the use of government. Social solidarity results in part from our allegiance to or connection with what Nisbet and others have called the "buffer" or "mediating" institutions. The family, the church, the voluntary association are examples of these intermediate entities that stand between the individual and the society as a whole (Nisbet 1975; Berger and Berger 1983; Novak 1980). But as government in this century has assumed many of the functions previously the province of the buffer institutions, social solidarity has diminished. For while it is possible for the individual to maintain strong sentiments of attachment to a large and impersonal government, without the mediating influences of the buffer institutions the sense of social solidarity eventually diminishes drastically.

The impact of all three of these factors has generated changes in the nature of work.

## THE CONSEQUENCES OF WEAKENING
## SOCIAL SOLIDARITY

The best indicators of the degree of social solidarity present in a society are the extent of trust and loyalty people feel toward a) other people and b) various institutions. There are two meanings to the word "trust." Both imply belief that the person or institution will meet our expectations in some specific way and that their behavior will be in our interest. The first usage refers to the expectation of competence in the successful completion of a task. The second refers to the moral aspect of the expectation, that is, the person or institution will act in such a way as not to violate some important implicit or explicit agreement made between us, or breach some universal norm.

There has been a significant diminution of the second variety of trust in the workplace. Part of it results from the use of a particular form of entrepreneurialism, and part is associated with the intrusion of government into the relationship between employer and employee.

In the past few years many companies have been managed by a strategy that Reich has called "paper entrepreneurialism" (Reich 1983). When business is oriented in this way the goal of the executives of the company is to earn as much short-term profits as possible. The achieving of long-range goals that require investment in research and development and large capital investments are given lower priority, since their pursuit may reduce immediate profits. Ironically, some of the pressure for quick profits comes from worker pension plans holding large blocks of shares in these companies and required to seek a maximum return on their investment (Drucker 1976).

"Paper entrepreneurialism" creates no new wealth: it merely redistributes wealth which already exists. It relies on manipulating quantified data in such a way that it indicates profitability (Reich 1983). New ways of accounting are devised that artificially raise profits. It is important that the price of shares be as high as possible, not only to satisfy the shareholders but to prevent takeovers by other paper entrepreneurs. There is a revolving door entry and exit of CEOs and other managers from firms. They leave because they are perceived as having failed in sufficiently appeasing the god of short-term profits, or they leave for some other company that makes them a better offer. The nature of these companies is further indicated by who sits on their Board of Directors. Whereas in Japan about 65 percent of those on Boards of Directors are educated as engineers, about the same percentage on the Boards of American firms are trained in law or accounting.

The other development in business that has reduced social solidarity among American workers and lower level executives is the internationalization of production and services. The United States has a history of the intramigration of a number of industries from one part of the country to another. One of the best-known examples was the move of furniture manufacturing plants from Northern locations such as Grand Rapids, Michigan to Southern sites such as North Carolina. Today, the move can be to any part of the world. Because of computerized telecommunications and rapid transportation, the entire firm does not have to be in one location; various plants and divisions can be set in many different locations. The motivation for this mobility is the availability of low-priced, hardworking labor, that is usually not unionized. Many companies believe they cannot compete without this geographical flexibility in an era of relatively free trade.

The consequence of paper entrepreneurialism and of company mobility is a growing sense of mistrust by the workers toward the companies that employ them. Workers and lower level managers believe they are much more likely today to lose their jobs or have their wages and benefits reduced by managers and directors practicing paper entre-preneurialism. Loss of a job is especially serious for the older worker, and even for younger workers there is an appreciable financial penalty (Bluestone and Harrison 1982). Inculcation of a sense of company loyalty becomes very difficult in this type of environment, and the chances of achieving it are even further reduced when workers observe that many of the upper level executives of the firm are careerists with no real sense of loyalty themselves.

In Japan, by contrast, these kinds of problems have been largely alleviated, for the skilled workforce at least, who are assured of job tenure. In Western Europe, too, the extreme U.S. pattern of mobility and paper entrepreneurialism is rare.

## THE INTRUSION OF GOVERNMENT
## AND SOCIAL SOLIDARITY

Since the 1890s the federal government of the USA has increasingly enlarged its say on what is appropriate in the workplace. Government regulation began with control of child labor. Then in the 1930s, it provided the mechanism which allowed the ascendancy of labor unions. And in recent years it has promulgated laws that deal with such wider matters as health and safety, pension plan protection, and maternity leave.

Few will doubt that many of these laws represented a step forward—but there was a price to be paid for governmental intrusion. Issues that had been negotiated between workers and employers were now mandated and enforced by the state. Such centrally designed rules simply cannot take account of local conditions.

That there are other ways to achieve the same purposes, and probably more effectively, is illustrated by the different ways the American and Swedish governments sought to ensure a safe and healthy environment. In the U.S. the government passed the Occupational Health and Safety Act and a government agency was entrusted to carry out its enforcement. In Sweden, workers actively collaborate with management to ensure a safe place of work. In the first scenario social solidarity is weakened; in the second, it is strengthened (Kasperson 1983).

The second consequence of government regulation was that workers began to use litigation to obtain redress for alleged harms in the workplace instead of using union intervention or some other more personal form of action. Trust between employees and managers (and even in certain situations between employee and employee) must significantly decline when everyone becomes wary of being the target of litigation. In order to avoid conflict which might eventually involve legal action, behavior becomes more defensive and less straightforwardly oriented to honest work goals.

## COMPUTER CONTROL AND DESIGN

The term 'industrial revolution' refers to a period characterized by the invention, construction, adoption and implementation of energy-driven technology which replaces the production of goods or services by artisanship, handcraft or simple clerical skills. The technological norm that organized these efforts was that of 'efficiency', that is, accomplishing a task by some combination of the least cost, the least effort, in the shortest time.

At the end of the nineteenth century Frederick Taylor devised the "Scientific School of Management," often called Taylorism. Its major goal was to increase the control of managers over workers and the manufacturing process. This was achieved by describing in detail every element of work procedures, by setting up timetables for the completion of tasks, and by establishing methods of monitoring and inspecting the quality and quantity of the subproduct and the finished product.

Perhaps the best-known of Taylor's ideas was that of breaking work down into smaller parts. A product that had previously been produced by the work of a few men was now produced by many more workers, each one undertaking a very small part of the total process (Friedmann 1955). This reduced the level of skill and education required of workers. Workers were easily replaced if their performance was unsatisfactory. Breaking work down into smaller parts made possible greater control by managers over the manufacturing (or service) process. The introduction of the assembly line was the ultimate in work rationalization in this sense.

In the factories using some version of the "Scientific Management" approach, it was an everyday sight to observe men with stopwatches conducting time and motion studies of

7

all sections of the work process, from the skilled work of a precision machinist to the tasks of the unskilled worker on the assembly line. These studies were intended to find out either the time it should take to perform a task, or, where a work norm had already been established, whether workers were meeting or exceeding the norm.

According to the earlier versions of Scientific Management, the employee was attached to work exclusively for economic reasons. He could be treated impersonally without consideration for such factors as loyalty and morale. In this conception, the worker was merely an extension of the machine and could be engineered in a similar fashion. But the reality of the actual operation of the plant was somewhat different from that envisaged by the planners.

In the average manufacturing plant there were various subgroups: managers and planners; highly skilled craftsmen such as tool and die makers; skilled workers such as precision machinists; semi-skilled workers; unskilled workers on the assembly line; and ancillary staff such as janitors and laborers. In addition, there were a large number of white collar workers, most of whom were not directly involved with the production process.

The most difficult of the blue collar workers to 'Taylorize' were the highly skilled. Their skill came from a combination of experience and personal qualities—and managers could find no way to rationalize these jobs to any significant extent. Moreover, since skilled craftsmen usually possess a high degree of occupational identity and often express independent sentiments about their work environment, managers using Taylor's approach found it difficult and indeed counterproductive to limit the discretion of skilled workers in how they did their work.

The assembly line work was the obvious focus for the most intensive efforts at rationalization of work tasks, and it was more successful than with skilled work. Despite the efforts of managers to create close to total control over the assembly line, there were even here a number of factors that limited their ability to accomplish this goal completely. The first is the human relations factor.

Despite the most strenuous efforts of planners to make the worker an extension of the machine and as predictable, workers adopted a number of methods to deflect or defeat the full achievement of these goals. Since the 1930s, industrial sociologists and researchers in business management have documented the creation of an informal social system among workers, whose activities are at variance with or even opposed to the goals enunciated by the leaders of the formal system (Rothlisberger and Dickson 1939; Homans 1950; Dalton 1959).

These researchers shared the view that Taylorism had overestimated the degree to which behavior on the job was motivated by consideration of pay and job security. According to this alternative perspective, people do better and more work on the job when they feel appreciated by their employer and by their fellow workers, when the work situation encourages feelings of social solidarity in the accomplishment of work tasks, and when there is more open communication at all levels of the work hierarchy. These doctrines led to the establishment of the "Human Relations" approach for industrial management. Along with "Scientific Management," this has been the dominant mode of work management in the twentieth century.

**THE COMPUTER**

It had long been a goal among business people to make automatic some of the discrete actions that were linked sequentially in production and service. From the nineteenth century onward—and in rudimentary form even earlier—there were some simple forms of automation available, for example, in the form of mechanical-electrical servomechanisms. This type of analog device which operates on the feedback principle was to become, during and after World War II, quite sophisticated and reliable (Rips 1990).

But they are primitive in both type and scope compared to the automatic processes of today. The invention of the transistor and advances in applied mathematics made possible the design and construction of the early computer. Advances in microchip development made feasible the miniaturized microcomputers of today. Compare the machines of today with the earlier massive banks of machines that occupied a large room and were serviced by "computer priests" in white coats, and one has an idea of the scale of the change which miniaturization has made possible.

The purchase price of the mechanical calculators that were used for computation in business and the academic world in the late 1950s, in terms of today's money, was more than four thousand dollars. They were noisy, about the size of a typewriter and prone to breakdown. Today's electronic calculator is reliable; it is silent, it can do more mathematical functions, and it can be held in the palm of the hand. Moreover, it can be purchased for as little as eight dollars.

Accompanying any significant development in technology, there are usually important changes in the nature of human relations in the workplace. Introduction of the assembly line mode of industrial production limited the variety of ways assembly line employees related to each other. Since each worker was a small, discrete part of the workline, and the nature and rhythm of the process was not under his control, communication between workers was not part of the design, and was in fact discouraged.

The workplace, which utilizes the computer for informational and operational purposes, can be organized in many different ways (Shaiken 1984). It *can* be used to achieve the ultimate dream of the contemporary Taylorite of almost total control of the work process. In this kind of design, according to Shaiken, there are basically two kinds of jobs. The first are the creative jobs at the top. These are the people who plan the process and design the means for computerized operation. The second group are those who merely monitor the machines and may perform minor adjustments in the process. This kind of organization goes far beyond the dreams of the earlier proponents of Scientific Management. This newer version of Taylorism also affects the management part of the organizational pyramid.

First, it makes possible the elimination of some middle and lower level management. What their duties were before are now subsumed (at least theoretically) by informational systems that can be monitored from a central source. Even designing new products and the modification of existing ones will be increasingly influenced. The existence of Computer Assisted Design (CAD) which allows simulation and specification of the whole design process with reduced assistance from skilled workers can also dramatically increase the process of centralization. Even such highly skilled jobs as tool and die work are being altered because of CAD. Where this system is in operation, the tool and die worker may no longer control the process. Instead, he now has the much reduced role of carrying out a highly detailed set of instructions.

Responses to the introduction of computer-controlled operations by workers vary according to the level of skill previously required. The highly skilled workers will most likely respond negatively to the de-skilling of their jobs. On the other hand, less skilled workers may welcome the replacement of traditional machines by those that are computer controlled.

As Shaiken points out, there are alternative ways the strengths of computer control and design can be used in service and manufacturing. A decentralized system can be created which allows more autonomy and collaboration between managers and workers. One of the crucial components of this kind of arrangement is that almost everyone involved at all stages in the process has access through the computer to relevant information. This approach allows each person to contribute his/her skill and inside knowledge to improving the product. Where computer processed information is shared with both managers and workers, the employee is an active participant in the manufacturing or service operation (Shaiken 1984).

In a sense, this represents a new and more advanced version of the Human Relations Approach. Its purpose is not only to raise the morale of workers, but also to make use of positive worker brainpower. This approach is different from many of the so-called "job enrichment" programs of the past twenty years. The typical arrangement in these earlier efforts was to group workers in teams. But the team production of, say, several hundred automobile engines can be deadly monotonous and stressful, and the workers may prefer to go back to the assembly line where the work is monotonous but less complicated (Goldmann 1979).

It is likely that in the computer era the Scientific Management mode of organization will continue to be used in mass manufacturing of simple items where skilled labor is unnecessary after the original design is made. But it is unclear which approach will become dominant in the twenty-first century in the manufacturing of more complex items or the provision of complex services.

The human relations systems so successfully used by the Japanese are unlikely to be adopted in toto in Western countries. The Japanese work environment stresses job stability, cooperation, consensus and obedience to authority on the part of the employee and a strong paternalism. In the West, there is frequent job changing and a sense of individualism that sets a limit on the degree of cooperation between workers and managers. The reciprocal factor of paternalism is absent in many companies.

Study of the competition over which mode of management will become predominant should be a primary focus of the sociology of work in coming decades. One important and interesting aspect of this study will examine the fate of the highly skilled worker in an era of computer-driven technology. Lewis Mumford wrote many years ago about the irretrievable loss of craft knowledge that occurred with the advance of the industrial revolution. Mumford believed that in the long run this loss diminished the quality of life (Mumford 1970). Will the advent of the computer accelerate this loss of knowledge?

There is one other development in work that has received considerable attention—worker ownership of plants. Part of this stems from the fact that many scholars of work harbor romantic-utopian sentiments toward workers owning and controlling their own workplace. Somehow capitalism is more palatable to these scholars if "the boss" is eased out of the picture. The feasibility of worker-takeover has been greatly enhanced by "paper entrepreneurialism." In this era of company takeovers and forced mergers, made possible by the use of large sums of borrowed capital, to protect themselves from negative consequences workers have organized to buy their company. Sometimes their goal is to create a totally worker-owned company. In some instances there is an attempt to go into partnership with some financial entity.

There are a number of serious problems to be solved if the worker-owned company is to be financially successful and satisfying to its workers. What is to be the nature of the management structure? It is unlikely that a classless society will be created in large firms. Some form of authority system will be necessary for the day-to-day operation of the plant. Its shape may very well resemble that found in the pri- vately-owned company. Second, how is disciplinary action against or termination of the worker-owner to be adminis- tered? And last, if the worker-owner wishes to leave the firm, what happens to his or her ownership assets? If it is in the form of stock shares, they cannot be sold on the open market without seriously compromising the nature of worker ownership.

There are some examples of successful ventures in worker ownership (Carnoy and Shearer 1980). But there are short-term and long-term factors that will limit this option. The crucial short-term factor is the decreasing availability of the large amounts of capital needed for purchase. The long-term factors include the nature of the present-day occupational career. Out of necessity and from preference, individuals make many job changes in the course of their working lives, more than previous generations have done. This limits identification with any one firm, and dampens desire for participation in worker ownership.

The nature of the modern economy also makes worker ownership of large businesses less attractive. In today's intensely competitive business environment, firms have adopted, in order to thrive or in some cases to survive, a flexible planning strategy. Outmoded plants may be closed, unprofitable divisions sold off, and some operations moved to other countries. This often entails the loss of a large number of jobs. Large worker-owner businesses are unlikely to be able to pursue this kind of flexibility. Even such revered experiments in worker ownership as the Israeli kibbutz are experiencing these problems (Brinkley 1989).

## SOCIAL SOLIDARITY: THE LABOR UNIONS

One of the most important developments in the area of work has been the continuing decline in the prevalence and importance of that key buffer institution and crucial instrument of solidarity–the labor union.

As the negotiator for wages and working conditions, focus for political activities, provider of economic, health and social services, and a common source for identity and identification, the labor union was the countervailing force that workers wielded against the attempts of employers to impose a model of pure capitalism. But now the labor unions are experiencing a period of decline, not only in the United States, but also in Western Europe and Japan.

The functional explanation for this decrease is that it is a result of the change from industrial economies to what Troy calls service-dominated economies (Troy 1986, 76). This changeover period has been marked by economic distress in the industrial sector, the layoff of workers, wage reductions agreed to by unions under the threat of plant closures, and a voluntary relinquishing by unions of their traditional adversarial relationship as a means of averting economic catastrophe for their members.

Another reason for the decline of unions is paradoxically the result of the success of organized labor in advancing its political agenda. Much of the legislation regarding worker health and safety, unemployment benefits, the vesting of pension funds, and worker rights within the firm have either become enacted into federal or state legislation or have been mandated by the courts. The presence of the union to win these gains for the workers through collective bargaining is no longer as important when they are now administered and enforced by governmental agencies.

But the decline in unionism has also been hastened, at least in the United States, by the perception that organized labor's leadership is interested primarily in furthering their own interests, and not in advancing the cause of the workers they represent (Lipset 1986, 299). Paradoxically, Lipset reports that the results of surveys show that Americans believe that labor unions are important and protect workers from mistreatment by employers–but that workers should not be required to join a union, or to pay dues so that they can work on a job (Lipset 1986, 316).

There are important consequences of declining union membership. One of the most significant relates to the wage structure of firms. In the unionized workplace there is typically greater equality of wages than in non-union establishments: in order to maintain social solidarity and to maximize benefits for the majority of their members, unions tend to limit the power of managers to set individual wage rates. The non-union company in the same industry is likely to have a wider range of wages, and gives a smaller percentage of compensation in the form of fringe benefits (Freeman 1986, 185).

Another important consequence of decreasing union membership is the creation of a different relationship between the workers and the managers. In the United States and the United Kingdom, especially in large companies, the union was often the advocate and mediator for the worker, right on the shop floor. The relationship between the workers and managers was structured to be adversarial but could be softened by good personal relationships.

Non-union companies, which wish to be profitable and avoid unionization, have to provide a more positive environment for the worker than is found in the union shop. This leads management to adopt a style that emphasizes an up-to-date version of the Human Relations Approach with good communication between all levels of employees, and demonstrate concern for the welfare of the worker. However, as discussed earlier, there are oppositional forces operating to reduce the effectiveness of the Human Relations Approach. The need of companies to maximize short-term profits, and achieve maximum flexibility in a situation of uncertainty commonly impels them to place these financial concerns ahead of concern for the worker. This aggravates the already difficult task of fostering trust and loyalty among employees.

In the large unionized company, during the golden age of unionism, workers often had a love-hate relationship with the company. But there was frequently a sense of what can be called 'antagonistic loyalty' felt by the worker toward the company. The worker, the union and the company were all an essential part of the setting where the drama of work was played out. All three were necessary for this adversarial relationship to be maintained. In the non-union firm this element is missing, and in an era when trust and solidarity are on the decline, it will be increasingly difficult to discover some alternative way of creating loyalty to the firm.

Despite setbacks in other areas, American labor unions have enjoyed considerable success in recent years in organizing one large sector of jobs—government workers. The enrollment of large numbers of government employees (including teachers) in labor unions began in the early 1960s and peaked in the mid-1970s. Although there has been somewhat of a drop in numbers since that time, the decline has been much slower than has occurred in the private sector. But because of the severe economic problems of municipal, state and federal governments, the influence of these unions, despite their still considerable political clout, will most likely decline in the coming years.

Does unionism have a future in the world of an increasingly globalized economy, where sentiments of social solidarity will be less valued than in the past, and where the increasing importance of the computer is altering the nature of work, itself? The growth of the trade unions in the nineteenth and twentieth centuries was partially a response to the rapid expansion of an economic and engineering -management system where the workers felt they did not have any appreciable influence over the amount of pay they received or their working conditions. Also, unions assumed an important role during a political era when reformist and collectivist political movements were becoming increasingly popular. The political climate is quite different today. People in many parts of the world are rejecting collectivism as a way of life. Reformism of the welfare state variety—what the writer has elsewhere termed "authoritarian liberalism" (Himelson 1975), is still an important political influence; but its agenda is limited to economic and social problems that appear to be intractable of solution by any other alternative. It is no longer the approach of preference, but of last resort.

But the worker's need to exercise some influence over economic factors and working conditions still remains—even in a new computer-guided work environment. The shape of the unions of the future that will attempt to meet these needs will most likely arise in response to new circumstances. With the exception of the job shop, the managers and workers of the past stayed at the same firm for long periods, often their entire working years. The trend today is for people to be more mobile. This is especially the case for managers, planners, programmers, and highly skilled workers. In the new computer-oriented work situation there is an apparent upgrading of jobs into management, for example, programmers.

These employees are no longer considered blue collar workers, but they are not members of a recognized profession, such as engineering. The growth in the number of such jobs may well lead to the creation of proto-professional associations that will work to enhance the status of these positions. Because these groups will be halfway between the model of a classical profession and a trade union, they will, like the labor union, act as a buffer between these employees and the employer in matters of salary and work conditions, and will act as a profession by attempting to control who is qualified to practice the occupation. Professional status will also reduce problems associated with increased job mobility. In contrast to the labor unions of the past, these associations will not be concerned with political matters that do not directly involve bread and butter issues concerning their own occupation.

What of the future of the mass labor union and the union movement as a political and economic force? Unions will not vanish: but structural and political trends in the foreseeable future appear to predict a further erosion of union strength. The shift of job opportunities from industry to services will probably result in a further decrease in the percentage of the labor force who are members of labor unions. (See The Hudson Institute's *Workforce 2000* for one prediction of the future labor market.)

A rise in the number of part-time or time-shared jobs, replacing full-time positions, will also have a dampening effect on union membership. And the dramatic rise in the number of women working full time will not lead to more members either. With some exceptions, women have been more reluctant than men to identify with organized labor, and will continue to be reluctant to join.

While labor is not winning the "numbers game," many unions have become a partner to dramatic changes in the way workers and managers relate to each other. This has particularly occurred in such mass production industries as the automobile industry. The industry experienced a traumatic drop in car sales during the 1970s and 1980s. This resulted in wage reductions, layoffs and plant closings. One of the major complaints about the American automobiles of this period was that their quality was substantially lower than imports, and especially in comparison with Japanese vehicles (Halberstam 1986). Both the companies and the union were threatened by the turndown and looked to each other for help in reversing the downward slide. This led to the establishment in 1987 of joint labor-management committees whose purpose was to improve the quality of the cars and the economic health of the firms (Keller 1989). These committees were modeled after similar units in Japan where they are claimed to have been successful in creating a more contented workforce and better cars. (See Sibney 1982 for a general view of the Japanese approach.)

It is too early to know if this new form of solidarity will prove to be successful in the automobile industry. But these changes will have a lasting impact on future relationships.

## LACK OF SOLIDARITY: THE UNDERCLASS

Bertrand Russell wrote, "I think there is far too much work done in the world, that immense harm is caused by the belief that work is virtuous and that what needs to be preached in modern industrial countries is quite different from what always has been preached...." What Russell appears to be railing against was not that some work is necessary for our existence, but rather that modern societies have to create a special morality regarding work in order to motivate people to spend so many hours working to accomplish so many tasks that are unnecessary in the first place. Russell, whether intentionally or not, was presenting an alternate view to those social philosophers of the nineteenth and twentieth centuries who assessed the social worth of people by how hard they worked and how productive their efforts were. Their special targets for disapproval were what they felt to be a parasitic aristocracy and a bloated and degenerating capitalist class (Veblen 1934).

A review of contemporary discourse regarding work shows how different is the population of concern today. It is not the aristocrat or capitalist who has gained our attention but those at the other end of the economic spectrum entirely—namely people identified as members of the 'underclass'. As Auletta points out, those who have studied poverty conclude that the underclass are not always poor (e.g., criminals), although most are; but what distinguishes them from others is that they "usually operate outside the generally accepted boundaries of society. They are often set apart...by their 'deviant' or anti-social behavior, by their bad habits, not just their poverty" (Auletta 1982, 28).

They differ from the immigrant poor who inhabited the tenements of the cities a century ago or even forty years ago. The majority do not live in two- parent families. Children are born to and raised by single women, many of whom were adolescents when they had their first child. The presence of men in these domiciles is usually transitory. The basic means of support for these women is from public assistance. There is a great deal of transgenerational poverty; that is, girls born into this situation recapitulate their mothers' lives when they reach adolescence. Although many are dissatisfied with their situation, they see no alternative way of life open to them because of their limited education, lack of knowledge of alternatives, or in some cases because of a masochistic satisfaction with a life that does not make unknown demands on them. In recent years, the widespread use of drugs has led to further deterioration of the life chances of people in this environment.

Many of the men in this group work only sporadically at legitimate employment; they may earn money by fringe activities or in clearly illegal endeavors. Some may temporarily earn large sums of money through crime, but their basic view of life remains that of a participant in the American version of the culture of poverty.

It is only within the last few years that the full dimensions of the problem of the underclass have been acknowledged by scholars of poverty and by the media. No longer was the claim made that simply giving people of this milieu more money would lead to upward mobility. It was now recognized that long-lasting changes could take place only if individuals received more formal education (academic and occupational) and adopted a set of attitudes that were more likely to aid them in improving their position in life. How to provide effective education for work and how to change attitudes regarding work and the work situation were central to any stratagem for promoting real change.

There are a number of obstacles that have reduced the possibility of change. The first involves the risk people take by moving from one status to another. In the United States, if a person remains on welfare he or she will receive, in addition to their monthly cash stipend, a rent subsidy, access to free medical care, food stamps and other government-provided services. For many, the alternative to welfare is a poor paying, uninteresting job that lacks all the ancillary benefits that comes with welfare status. One writer estimated that a family of four would have to earn sixty percent above minimum wage to get out of poverty (Graham 1988).

If there appears to be little chance for upward mobility, then they don't see any reason to take a risk and make the change. There would also be stronger motivation for risk-taking if there was social stigma associated with welfare status, as was the case in earlier decades. Instead, many rationalize the reasons for their situation by seeing themselves as a victim of "society," and therefore entitled to the payments they receive–as if they were securing reparations.

The second reason concerns the lack of skills of most persons in the underclass. At a time when the educational requirements for satisfying jobs is rising, educational achievements among persons in the underclass are falling. The high school dropout rate has risen precipitously.

The third obstacle to success is found within the person. It is the exhibiting of behavior that is dysfunctional to "making it" in the world of work. Specifically, these often include not being on time for work, not knowing how to, or not wanting to, deal satisfactorily with authority on the job. Inappropriate attire and grooming frequently arouses negative feelings in potential employers, and preclude the hiring of an otherwise acceptable job candidate.

Some of the other obstacles to employment are external. A significant number of persons in the underclass have criminal records. Considerable stigma attaches to this history and employers are more reluctant to hire people with this background (Himelson 1966). Also, racial and ethnic discrimination still do exist. But it is the *combination* of being from the underclass *and* being non-white that generates high levels of discrimination.

Since the mid-1960s there have been many job programs targeted on the underclass. The results of these efforts, like so many other endeavors of the period between 1965 and 1980 that were aimed at the same population, were negative or very modest in the improvement they produced. Job voucher programs in which the potential employer was offered a financial incentive to hire the applicant had poor results. The stigma attached to those in a program for the disadvantaged appear to outweigh the economic incentives.

More expensive programs are not necessarily more effective in achieving modest gains. Burtless, in summarizing the results of these projects states, "...nearly *all* manpower strategies for the disadvantaged, including those that are far more expensive than job search training, share the same characteristic; they raise the amount of time that workers spend employed, but have little effect on their hourly rate" (Burtless 1984, 22). Another interesting finding is that the more ambitious programs such as those operated by the Manpower Development Research Corporation helped welfare mothers, but not ex-convicts, former drug addicts and high school dropouts (Burtless 1984, 22).

Should we be satisfied with these modest results which benefit only a handful of individuals or should we strive to construct more effective programs that reach more people? Given the state of governmental budgets today, can we find inexpensive ways of getting persons in the underclass into employment, out of dependency and away from deviant behavior?

Today, governments and their citizens search for ways to raise up those at the bottom of the social and economic ladder. This is partly out of concern for the health and safety of the larger society, but equally out of a real concern for the condition of fellow human beings and compatriots. Compare this attitude to one expressed about a similar population, over 140 years ago, "...the social scum, that passively rotting mass thrown off by the lowest layers of the old society...." This was Karl Marx speaking of what he called the "lumpenproletariat" (Marx 1970).

Any strategy designed to bring more people from the underclass into regular and continuous employment will have to take into consideration several aspects of the problem. First, for there to be any significant movement of large numbers of people from dependency to self-sufficiency and employment, a carrot-and-stick approach will have to be adopted and utilized. The beginnings of this are seen in the workfare programs which have been recently instituted in the U.S. after the passage by the Congress of a welfare reform bill.

Probably even more important are measures to reduce in number the potential recruits for a new generation of underclass. (See Segalman and Himelson, 1984 for a discussion of such strategies.)

Second, the stigma adhering to vocational training must be removed. Forty years ago there were a number of excellent vocational high schools throughout the United States. But they began to disappear in the 1960s after protests by minority rights organizations, sensitive to old stereotypes, that children attending these schools were being labeled as "dumb" and therefore not of college caliber. But there are many students who might have attended these vocational schools who will never seriously attend a college or university. Instead, many of them became dropouts from secondary schools for lack of interest. While it is unrealistic to believe that vast numbers of children of the underclass would complete these programs, if even a significant minority of them learned occupational skills or some trade that is in demand, this would be a sizeable step forward. Vocational programs can also have another benefit; they provide adult, male role models, in the person of the vocational instructor. Boys who have grown up in homes that are without men who work in regular occupations, would have the opportunity to learn about work from the instructor.

The third point is in regard to the locus and size of programs. The evidence from the evaluation of job programs in the U.S. tends to indicate that smaller sized programs may be more effective than larger ones in recruiting candidates and placing them in jobs after training. It is possible that small locally run and funded projects may be better at preparing people for employment than are large-scale bureaucratically managed organizations that are more remote from local conditions. More experimentation with localism is called for.

The next point is last but not least. The notion that there is no point in taking a "dead-end job" must be counteracted, not in this case because someone is needed to do the work, but because for most of the underclass, *this is the only way to get started to move upward.* For a person with minimal skills, and lacking formal education, the creation of an employment biography that demonstrates reliability, honesty and job competence is an essential step to getting a better job. Even though each of the "dead-end jobs" by themselves lead nowhere, they are the first step in the compilation of this biography. Some political liberals and welfare rights activists did a great disservice when they stigmatized these jobs and claimed it was preferable to go on welfare.

## THE SHAPE OF THE FUTURE

Barring political or economic cataclysms, the nature and extent of solidarity in work in the future will be very different from that prevalent in the twentieth century. Those factors which helped create strong social solidarity in work, such as trust and loyalty, are diminishing, and with them such mediating institutions as the labor union. The autonomous, flexible, mobile employee is becoming the model of the future. Because of computer associated technology there will be great opportunities for certain kinds of creativity, especially for the university educated. What the role will be for the skilled craftsman is uncertain. In firms that use the computer to enlarge employee participation, they will have a reliable niche. In those that try to push Taylorism to its limits, their future is much less certain. But experience indicates that even in these firms the managers cannot totally eliminate skilled jobs without negative consequences (Shaiken 1984).

The prospects for semi-skilled and unskilled workers are much bleaker. The new technology is eliminating industrial jobs. New jobs will be available in the service area for some of those so displaced. What their wages will be is problematic, but it seems likely they will be lower than they were receiving for industrial work.

With the decreasing membership and importance of labor unions, worker solidarity is weakened and their bargaining position, whether in industrial or service work, becomes enfeebled. Our prediction is that workers will strengthen their position by creating a new form of mass worker organizations that will be based on geography rather than function. Thus, unskilled industrial workers will be members of the same organization as service employees. If they move from one job to another they will remain in the same organization. This organization (union if you will) will be the negotiator and lobbyist for the worker.

# REFERENCES

Auletta, Ken. *The Underclass.* New York: Random House. 1982.

Bluestone, Barry and Bennett Harrison. *The Deindustrialization of America.* New York: Basic Books. 1982.

Brinkley, Jose. "Debts make Israelis rethink an ideal: the Kibbutz" *New York Times International Edition.* 6.

Burtless, Gary. "Manpower policies for the disadvantaged: What works." *Brookings Review* vol. 3 no. 1. Fall 1984. 18-22.

Dalton, Melville. *Men Who Manage.* New York: Wiley. 1959.

Carnoy, Martin and Derek Shearer. "Democratizing the work place" in *Economic Democracy,* Martin Carnoy, ed. White Plains, NY: M.E. Sharpe. 1980.

Drucker, Peter. *The Unseen Revolution.* New York: Harper and Row. 1976.

Durkheim, Emile. *The Division of Labor in Society.* New York: The Free Press. 1956.

Freeman, Richard. "Effects on the economy" in *Unions In Transition.* Seymour Martin Lipset, ed. San Francisco: ICS Press. 1986. 177-200.

Friedmann, Georges. *Industrial Society.* New York: The Free Press. 1955.

Gibney, Frank. *Miracle By Design.* New York: Times Books. 1982.

Goldmann, Robert. "Six automobile workers in Sweden" in *American Workers Abroad.* Robert Schrank, ed. Cambridge, MA: MIT Press. 1979.

Halberstam, David. *The Reckoning.* New York: William Morrow & Co. Inc. 1986.

Himelson, Alfred. "Criminal rehabilitation" in *Understanding Social Problems.* D. Zimmerman and D.L. Wieder, eds. Praeger. 1976.

_____. *Risk and Rehabilitation: An Employment Study.* Sacramento, CA: Institute for the Study of Crime and Delinquency. 1966.

Homans, George. *The Human Group.* New York: Harcourt Brace & Co. 1950.

Hudson Institute. *Workforce 2000.* Indianapolis, IN. 1987.

Kasperson, Roger. "Worker participation in protection: the Swedish alternative". *Environment* vol. 25, no. 4. 1983.

Keller, Maryann. *Rude Awakening: The Rise, Fall and Struggle for Recovery of General Motors.* New York: Morrow. 1989.

Lipset, Seymour Martin. *Unions in Transition.* San Francisco, CA: ICS Press. 1986.

_____. "Labor unions in the public mind" in Lipset, op. cit. 1986. 287-321.

"Making a case for unions". *Los Angeles Times.* August 13, 1989. 3.

Marx, Karl. *The Communist Manifesto.* New York: Pathfinder Press. 1970.

Mumford, Lewis. *The Myth of the Machine: The Pentagon of Power.* New York: Harcourt, Brace and Jovanovich. 1970.

Nisbet, Robert. *The Twilight of Authority.* New York: Oxford University Press. 1975.

Novak, Michael. *Democracy and Mediating Structures.* Washington, D.C.: American Enterprise Institute. 1980.

Reich, Robert. *The Next American Frontier.* New York: Times Books. 1983.

## WORK AND EMPLOYMENT

Rips, Jules. Personal Interview, Los Angeles, CA. April 1990.

Roethlisberger, F.J. and W.J. Dickson. *Management and the Worker.* Cambridge, MA: Harvard University Press. 1939.

Russell, Bertrand. *In Praise of Idleness.* London: George Allen & Unwin.

Segalman, Ralph and Himelson, Alfred. "Strategies for welfare reform". *The Futurist.* vol. 18, no. 5. October 1984.

Shaiken, Harley. *Work Transformed: Automation and Labor in the Computer Age.* New York: Holt, Rinehart and Winston., 1984.

Taylor, Frederick. *Principles of Scientific Management.* New York: Harper and Row. 1911.

Tocqueville, Alexis de. *Democracy in America.* New York: Harper and Row. 1966.

Troy, Leo. "The rise and fall of American trade unions" in Lipset, *op.cit.* 1986. 75-109.

Veblen, Thorstein. *The Theory of the Leisure Class.* New York: Modern Library (Random House). 1934.

Weber, Max. *From Max Weber: Essays in Sociology.* Hans Gerth and C. Wright Mills, eds. New York: Oxford University Press. 1946.

# CHAPTER 2

# THE NINETEENTH CENTURY WORKER: EXPLOITED SLAVE, OR THE LAST FREE MAN?

*John Chodes*

Today national governments control most aspects of inter-personal relationships in the workplace, via a host of laws which focus on sex and age discrimination, sexual harassment, equal opportunities, non-discriminatory hiring and firing practices, and so on. All this law spells out formally the behavior between employer and worker and worker to worker in minute detail. To put it simply, the workplace is being nationalized. A bureaucrat is now our manager of record, not our immediate boss.

The seeds for absorbing private enterprise into the State began early in the nineteenth century as the industrial revolution emerged. As it did, a great hue-and-cry went up about the horrendous conditions that the workers supposedly struggled against: 14-hour days, children having their youth destroyed by starvation wages and dangerous conditions, squalid and disease-spreading living quarters. And when they were used up they were thrown on the scrap heap. Retirement? Forget it. They worked until they fell down dead.

It all sounds like a cancer that was cured by government's stringent controls. Under this scenario, nationalization makes perfect sense. But it is patently false. It was politically motivated propaganda concocted by the British aristocracy fearful of losing their traditional status. Their objective was to crush the rising manufacturing class who were threatening their powers. In the thirty years after the invention of the steam engine (1760), a spate of inventions transformed spinning into a factory process. British history had ceased to be the story of a small ruling class. "The ancient feeling of contempt by the country gentlemen toward the burghers, still seems to rankle in the breasts of many members of our aristocracy...and displayed itself in the Parlimentary crusade against the factories" (Ure 1835, 277).

To gain support for this crusade, the Tories (representing the aristocrats) invoked the idyllic "Romantic" view of pre-industrial England. This contrasted the horrors of the satanic mills with the perfect earlier age. The Communist revolutionary, Friedrich Engels, echoed the conservative view: "Before the introduction of machinery in the textile industry, the spinning and weaving of materials took place in the home of the workers...most of the weavers lived in the country near to a town and earned enough to live on...In those days the weaver had as much free time as he wanted because he could arrange his hours of work on the loom to suit his own convenience...the workers enjoyed a comfortable and peaceful existence. They were righteous, God-fearing and honest. Their standard of life was much better than that of the factory worker today. They were not forced to work excessive hours...Their children grew up in the open air of the countryside and if they were old enough to help their parents work, this was an occasional employment and there was no question of an 8 or 12-hour day" (Engels 1958, 10).

That was the dream. Then Engels stumbles onto the true pre-industrial master-slave reality: The weavers "regarded the Squire, the most important landlord in the district, as their natural superior...they were not troubled by intellectual or spiritual problems. They could seldom read or write. They took no interest in politics, never concerned themselves with the problems of the day...yet they remained in some respects little better than beasts of the field. They were not human beings at all but human machines in the service of a small aristocratic class which had hitherto dominated the life of the country...the industrial revolution...forced the workers to think for themselves and demand a fuller life in human society" (ibid., 12).

In that mythc "Golden Age," the workers were exploited ruthlessly by the aristocrats but were hidden from view in isolated rural workshops.

Our story focuses on England rather than the USA or other major industrialized nations because "The early British factory system forecast the trend of subsequent industrial development and judgements passed upon it then, largely determine the attitude taken with regard to the modern industrial system...Factory legislation the world over has been framed on British models" (Hayek 1954, 156).

By the 1830s in England, there were twice as many urban workers in manufacturing and trade than agriculture. The USA lagged far behind. Farm work dominated America, where the first power loom was used in 1814, over half a century after Britain.

## THE SADLER COMMITTEE:
## EXPLOITATION OR IMMORALITY

The first Parliamentary factory commissions focused on women and children. The classic Sadler Committees are one of the main sources for early factory life. The first, in 1831, was so biased against the mill owners that even its supporters were embarrassed. Sadler presented a dreary picture of immorality, cruelty and deformity. Yet even Friedrich Engels admitted: "The Report was emphatically partisan, composed of strong enemies of the factory system, for party ends. Sadler permitted himself to be betrayed by his noble enthusiasm into the most distorted and erroneous statements" (Hayek 1954, 160).

Sadler used evidence from former times as if the abuses were current. The evidence was not given under oath. It was found to be "absolutely false" (ibid., 159).

Sadler created the Committee to fight for the "Ten Hours Bill," apparently to limit children's working time. But the Bill put urban factories under the control of rural lawmakers. The Committee also seemed less concerned with the charges of worker exploitation than with the "immorality" of their newly elevated standard of living.

Immorality was defined as: "Children were no longer contented with plain food but had to have dainties" (ibid., 171). Or: "The tendency of girls to buy clothes instead of making them, which makes them unfit for motherhood" (ibid., 171). Or: "The pocketbook makers have high wages...hence they are very dissipated" (ibid., 172).

Engels echoed the Commmittee: In the "manufacture of bobbin lace large numbers of young people are employed. They receive virtually no moral training. They also love fine clothes. These factors combine to lower their moral standards to such an extent that prostitution is almost universal among them" (Engels 1958, 218).

Morality (or more accurately, values control) was the impulse for the Committee from the beginning. A highly influential book, *The Manufacturing Population of England,* by Dr. Peter Gaskell, pushed the Tories toward regulation. The book seemed to concentrate on the worker's starvation wages. Yet Gaskell conceded that with proper economy, industrial wages "would enable them to live comfortably, nay, in comparative luxury." Gaskell condemned factories "for their vice, where children are forced to spend their most impressionable years in utmost immorality and degradation" (Hayek 1954, 167).

Yet Commissioner Tufnel, in his report to the Secretary of State, said: "The whole current of testimony goes to prove that the charges made against cotton factories on the grounds of immorality—are calumnies" (ibid., 158).

## WOMEN AND CHILDREN LIBERATED

The issue of morality was raised because the factory system had revolutionary implications. It made women and children independent. Engels: "When children earn more than the cost of their keep, they make contributions to the family budget and keep the rest as pocket money...Often this occurs when they are no more than 14 or 15. In brief, the children become emancipated and regard their parents' house merely as lodging, and quite often, if they feel like it, they leave home and take lodgings elsewhere...when (they) are the sole breadwinners in families where the parents are unemployed, the children rule the household" (Engels 1958, 162-165).

Lord Ashley gave an example of this in a speech to the House of Commons on March 15, 1844, stating that an unemployed father rebuked his daughters for frequenting a public house. They turned on him, saying that they no longer recognized his authority. "Damn you, we have you to keep!" They said they were entitled to spend at least part of their earnings as they pleased (ibid., 165).

Engels: "The fact that a married woman is working (leads) to a reversal of the normal division of labor within the family. The wife is breadwinner while her husband stays at home to look after the children and do the cleaning and cooking. This deprives the husband of his manhood and the wife of all womanly qualities" (ibid., 162,164).

Women's incomes did have enormous social impact. In an 1844 study of 43 cotton mills in Manchester, employing

17,235 people, 51 percent were women (Ure 1835, 307). In a similar study in Lancaster, Massachusetts, 85 percent were women (Abott 1910, 90).

To those who despised the free market, these numbers indicated the displacement of higher paid men by exploited women. The opposite is true. Women were more appropriate for factory work since muscle power was no longer important. "When spinning or weaving machinery is installed, practically all that is left to be done by hand is the piecing together of broken threads and the machine does the rest. The task calls for nimble fingers rather than muscular strength. The labor of grown men is not merely unnecessary but actually unsuitable because the bones and muscles of their hands are more developed than those of women and children" (Engels 1958, 158). "In a modern factory...spinners spend part of their day reading (Ure 1835, 310).

Another common assumption is that women have always earned less than men for the same job. This idea needs reassessment. From a study of 43 Manchester mills, between 9 and 18 years, boys and girls earned virtually the same amount. Only when they matured was there a wage spread. For 18-21 year-olds, 10.4 shillings for men and 8.11 for women. Beyond 21, men earned 22.5, women 9.6 shillings (ibid., 307).

One reason for the wage differential is that women did not work as steadily as men. "The girls had come to work with their hands but that did not hinder the working of their minds also. Some of them were able to attend...school half of the year by working in the mills the other...Capable, ambitious girls did not stay long in the mills. They...came into the factory for perhaps a year or two, and then went home...to pay off a mortgage on the paternal farm or to earn money for her own education" (Abbott 1910, 117).

There are also many instances of women making more than men for the same jobs. This fact warranted an official report from the Inspector of Factories in 1843: "There is at present a very anomolous state of things in regard to wages in some departments of cotton mills in Lancashire. There are hundreds of young men, between 20 and 30 years of age, in the full vigor of life, employed as piercers and otherwise, who are receiving not more than 8 or 9 shillings a week; while under the same roof...young women between 16 and 20 are getting 10 to 20 shillings per week" (Engels 1958, 158).

The strongest impulse for legislating the mills centered on children. The popular image is that they worked 14 hours a day, earned a pittance, were abused by the foremen and grew old before they matured. This is Tory propaganda.

First, few children worked *in* factories and fewer were employed *by* them. An 1881 Toronto study of 43,511 factory workers revealed that only 175 children under 10 were employed (Cross 1974, 74).

An 1844 study of 412 Lancaster factories with 116,281 workers, showed that only 3.2 percent were under 13 years old (*Manchester Guardian* 1844). And: "Nearly all children under 14 belong to the mule spinner department" (Ure 1835, 290). They worked on a machine called the "slubber," piecing raw fibers together. This was the last factory process to be automated. One adult slubber generally had 4 pieceners working for him. "These pieceners were not employed by the factory but by the slubber. The slubber is an independent workman, paid by the piece, not time. The slubber is often the father of the pieceners...If a child fails to join the fibers together, the ends are said to be 'let up', resulting in a delay in the work. Complaints of child abuse take place between the slubber and his pieceners. As overseer, the slubber is often at the nearest pub and when he returns he may be in an evil humor" (ibid., 295).

Factory Commission testimony confirmed this:

Question: Who is it that beats the children?
Answer: The slubber.

# WORK AND EMPLOYMENT

> Question: Not the master?
> Answer: No, the master has nothing to do with the children. They do not employ them.
>
> Question: Do you pay and employ your own pieceners?
> Answer: Yes.
>
> Question: Are the children ever beaten?
> Answer: Sometimes they get beat, but not severely. For sometimes they make the stuff to waste and their correction is needful. But that is unknown to the master. He does not allow beating at all (ibid., 300).

Automation of the slubber process, not legislation, largely ended the need for child labor.

Children did not work the same hours as adults. "When 9 years old, the child is sent to the factory where he or she works a 6.5 hour day...Some of the children only work when there is a breakdown. They do not know how long they will work, whether two hours or all night. This is a ready excuse for staying out all night" (Engels 1958, 169).

## WORKING HOURS COMPARABLE TO TODAY

To judge from the myths, it must have been exhausting to work in a nineteenth-century mill. Twelve to fourteen hours a day, year in, year out. The Factory Enquiry Commission of 1842 stated that the "framework stocking knitters were the worst paid of all the operatives in Leicester. They normally earned 6 shillings a week. Hours of work: 16 to 18 a day" (ibid., 214).

The Commission fudged the facts. They were not factory operatives. They were self-employed. The looms were hand-driven, in their homes. Buried in the report was the fact that they used to earn more but were hurt by modern machinery (ibid., 214).

This technique of combining the brutal conditions of non-industrial workers with the high paid factory hands was common in early commission reports. Yet the difference between the two systems is shown by a reporter who interviewed a clothing manufacturer whose employees worked from their homes. "Work is from 6 A.M. to 7 P.M. A man could make $11 a week, a girl, $5" (The Daily Mail and Express, 1897). This reporter entered a factory where the same work was being done by women. "Instead of wearing out their lives with a heavy (hand operated) machine, all the machines were run by electricity. The books showed that the average wage paid operatives was $10 a week and as high as $20. The shop did not open to the women till 8 A.M. and was generally closed by 6 P.M." (ibid.).

Unlike today, in the nineteenth century, worker loyalty hardly existed. Nor was it expected. The free market meant freedom for both sides. "Among the comparatively well-paid spinners, there were many who...were highly irregular in their attendance. A House of Lords Committee was told in 1818 that spinners frequently stayed off work without notice and then sent for their wages at the end of the week" (Aspin 1969, 37). And "one of the largest Manchester firms replaced spinners who were absent two or three hours after starting time on Monday, on the usually correct assumption that the men had left. Turnover of adult labor was 100 percent a year" (ibid., 37). And "the great manufacturing system is without doubt the first cause of all the workers arrogance...it is no unusual thing for a man, who, by a course of severe abstinance and industry, to collect a stock of cash, to retire altogether from his home and live for a fortnight at a public house, during the whole of which time his only concern is never to allow himself to get sober. When he has expended all his money, he will return to his employment and toil away resolutely and cheerfully...I have been informed by a proprietor of a manufacturing firm, that several of his most skillful lads were men who spent their time in these alterations of drunkenness and industry" (ibid., 37).

In addition, most work was seasonal. At peak periods, mills ran around the clock. Operatives had the option to work long hours and make as much as they could before "short time" or a complete mill shutdown gave them a long vacation. So, long hours were welcomed, not resented. "Every manufacturer is well acquainted with the eagerness of his spinners to earn the highest possible wages by quick work and prolonged hours and knows that if he stops his mill half an hour sooner than his neighbor, he will certainly lose his most skillful hands" (Ure 1835, 289). And, "in Lynn, the shoe industry has two annual seasons, each lasting 17 weeks. Women are given 2 to 4 days work as the season began, with a gradual increase to full time during the rush season" (Abbott 1910, 169).

There are sample working hours from Toronto in the 1880s, by trade, for women, based on a 6-day week. "Baking: 55 hours. Bookkeeping: 50-55 hours. Boots and shoes: 49. Binding and twine: 49-50. Corsets: 47-50. Envelopes: 53-55. Knitting: 54-55" (Cross 1974, 121). This is only slightly more than an 8-hour day in an unregulated work climate. In addition, "Many factories shut down from two to ten weeks in the winter" (ibid., 122). That would make their annual working hours less than many contemporary workers!

A Canadian Royal Commission in the 1880s questioned a coal company president:

Question: How many hours do (your miners) work?
Answer: They do piecework and they generally work about 10 hours.
Question: Are they constantly employed?
Answer: There are 4 months of the year when we are shut down (ibid., 79).

Also, "Fur workers and laborers mostly work 7 to 10 months of the year and averaged 50-56 hours a week when they worked" (ibid., 182).

The factory system also broke down the traditional class barriers, allowing workers to rise up via role models they never had before. "Men, sometimes wholly illiterate, have risen to profuse luxury which strangely contrasts with the primitive simplicity of their manners. Of course, it is the ambition of everyone to tread in their steps. *The man who has saved a little money, throws it into machinery or raises a weaving shop of his own*" (Aspin 1969, 83).

## URBAN BLIGHT NOT RELATED
## TO INDUSTRIALIZATION

Nineteenth century 'reformers' condemned the urban blight they connected with industrialization, believing free market greed created it. The following is typical. Reverend G. Alston of Bethnal Green, London, gives an account of his parish in the 1840s: "It contains 1,400 houses inhabited by 2,795 families (in a) space less than 400 yards and it is not uncommon for a man and his wife, with 4 or 5 children and sometimes the grandparents to be found living in a room 10 feet square, which serves them for eating and *working*." (They are not industrial operatives. They work at home.) "If we really desire to find *the most destitute* and deserving we must lift the latch of their doors." (Consistent with the Romantic spirit, extreme examples are presented as typical.) "There is not one father of a family in ten that possesses any clothes but his working dress—and that too commonly is in the worst tattered condition. And with many, this wretched clothing forms their only covering at night" (Engels 1958, 35). Another report stated: "Hens roost on the posts, while dogs and even horses sleep in the same room as human beings" (ibid., 42).

Horrible descriptions like these led Parliament toward regulation. It seemed to characterize the industrial workers. This is incorrect. It only depicted how non-industrial workers or recently arrived Irish immigrants lived. When the Irish left their poverty, they brought the rural lifestyle with them but did not have the skills yet for industrial employment. Even the 'reformers' eventually grasped this truth. Engels: "Hordes of (Irish) have flocked to Great Britain...nearly all settle in great cities where they form the lowest stratum of the community...the vast majority of the Irish (in Ireland) live in single-room cabins built of mud... Their...habits do no great harm in the countryside...(but) a dangerous situation... develops when such habits are practiced among the crowded population of big cities...emptying all their refuse out of the front door... (allowing the) pig to share their own sleeping quarters...a heap of straw and a few rags too tattered to wear, suffice for bedding" (ibid., 106).

Engels confirmed that such squalor was not related to industrial workers. "All occupations which demand little or no skill are open to the Irish...hand loom weavers, laborers, porters, odd-job men" (ibid., 107).

In describing the tightly packed, filthy and poorly drained quarters of the "industrial workers," Engels is actually revealing another underclass. "An endless labyrinth of narrow lanes... old towering houses crumble to decay, destitute of water, comprising 3 or 4 families—20 people in each flat. These districts are occupied by the poorest, most depraved and most worthless portion of the population. Thieving and prostitution are the main sources of income of these people" (ibid., 45,46).

This is not where the industrial workers live. In fact, the thieves and prostitutes lived in these decrepit buildings because "by law, no rent can be charged on them" (ibid., 47). The courts had condemned them.

Louis Rene Villerme, a French doctor, saw the worker's standard of living directly related to their behavior, not exploitation. He said that alcoholism, not low wages, was a major factor for poverty. In 1841 Villerme noted a great difference in living standards among workers earning the same wages. They organized themselves into "well behaved" and "badly behaved" sectors. The well-behaved group "does not always earn the best wages but they are clean, economical and especially sober. They house, clothe and feed themselves better...In Lille, with a mother, father and child working, they could save 50 to 100 francs a year—out of a 915-franc total household income, if they were prudent...The improvement of the worker's lot depends almost always on their own will... regulations on wages and conditions will not reduce poverty. The remedy is in realistic behavior...Industry and commerce are two great sources of liberty and civilization, not misery" (Stearns 1972).

## WAGES AND THE STANDARD OF LIVING

Enemies of free trade attached the factory system by fusing it to the impoverished non-industrial world. Yet the "yeoman and the laborer are both tempted from the plough. Who will work for 1 to 2 shillings a day at a ditch when he can get 3 to 5 in a cotton works and be drunk 4 days out of 7" (Aspin 1969, 35). That's 30 shillings a week. Those wages were called "beyond all imagination" (ibid., 36). During a boom, wages were even higher. In 1802 "there was never known so great an activity in the manufacture of Blackburn calicoes as at present...many weavers at this time are able, singly, to earn 45 to 50 shillings a week" (ibid., 36).

Non-industrial frame-stocking knitters who worked at home (in 1842) earned 6 shillings a week working 16 to 18 hours a day. They paid the price for being "too proud to answer the summons of the factory bell" (Engels 1958, 214).

These numbers are just abstractions until we know what they purchased. Here a coal company president responds to a Canadian inquiry board in the 1880s:

Question: What would the average wages of the (coal) cutters be?

Answer:     I think $1.50 would be the average, although
            some workers earn over $2 a day.

Question:   Does the company own the miner's houses?
Answer:     Yes.

Question:   What is the average rent?
Answer:     $2 to $2.50 a month (Cross 1974, 79,80).

This ratio of wages to rent is much lower than today. This same board asked a miner: "Do many men who work in your mine own houses?" He replied: "Yes. Quite a number."

This same board asked a doctor about the cost of food. "The cost of a meal will be about ¾ cent, (being) barley, cornmeal, red herring" (ibid., 165).

This board asked a bank accountant: "What classes of people are depositors?" He replied: "Working class. Laboring and mechanical classes are three-quarters of our customers.

Question:   What is the limit of deposit?
Answer:     $1,000. And a great many laboring people
            have reached it. They withdraw large amounts
            in the spring to buy a house or a piece of
            land...I know mechanics...who have all the
            comforts and conveniences that a great many
            professional men have not" (ibid., 178,179).

In the 1840s, in England, the average adult male mill operative made 22 shillings a week (Engels 1958, 154). In London, the most expensive city, he could rent a ground floor apartment in the center of the city for 4 shillings a week (ibid. 35).

In the 1890s, in Montreal, a poverty wage was $6 a week. A good 4-room apartment was $6 to $8 a month. Bread was 2.3 cents a pound, beef 6-12 cents a pound, potatoes 70 cents for 1.5 bushels. These prices are much lower, relatively, than now (Cross 1974, 59,180,181).

Finally, it was Engels who condemned the factory system because few operatives were over 40 years old. He concluded that overwork killed them off. Yet an 1843 study showed that "the percentage of persons above 40 engaged in mills is only 7.6 percent. This does not arise from superannuation (retirement) as from the number of mill hands who are enabled by their savings to enter into superior occupations. Of them, 197 have been traced (to) Ashton- under-Lyne...we find that 14 have become master spinners and manufacturers, 61 shopkeepers, 42 publicans and beer retailers, 11 grocers and tea dealers and the rest have found other respectable means of obtaining a livelihood" (*Manchester Guardian* 1843).

## HEALTH AND SAFETY OF INDUSTRIAL WORKERS

We have been taught to view the nineteenth century workplace as one of indifference and cruelty. Supposedly, if workers were laid off or hurt on the job they were in deep trouble, since no benefits existed for them. Crippling was widespread because of insuffieient safety precautions. Epidemics were transmitted via the crowded factories, which were built for profit, not human needs. But this perspective is incorrect. It is propaganda.

Again, Engels provides a clue to the true forces behind injury in the workplace: "The most unhealthy type of work is the grinding of knife blades and forks. Sharp metallic dust is thrown up into the air...attempts have been made to protect the grinders by covering the grinding wheels...but the grinders themselves are not in favor of these precautions and have sometimes destroyed the safety apparatus...they fear that if the trade becomes safer, it will attract more workers and so lead to a fall in wages. They believe in a 'short life but a merry one' " (Engels 1958, 231).

Engels also stated: "Accidents occur in rooms crammed full of machinery." Another view was presented by the

*Manchester Guardian* in 1844: "Out of upwards of 850 accidents occasioning loss of life, only 29 or 3.3 percent have been (by) factory machinery."

The editors of Engels' famous "Condition of the Working Class in England" point out the deceptions in his presentation of industrial accidents. Engels described how a 12-year-old had his hand crushed by machinery. He did not report that the boy "was employed in another part of the works and had no right to be touching the machinery in which his hand was trapped" (Engels 1958, 186).

The various commissions sought to prove that factory work deformed children. Yet, "All the deformed people produced before the Factory Commission were adults–there was no case advanced of a child deformed by work" (Ure 1835, p.402).

A Dr. Hawkins told the Factory Commission: "In the 16 years I have been physician to the Royal Infirmary I have put to the patient the question, previous to an operation, 'What trade are you of?', especially when the case was of a distorted limb. The answer has almost never been, 'Work in a cotton factory' but almost constantly, 'A hand-loom weaver'" (ibid., 377).

There was widespread deformity at the time, quite independent of occupation. Andrew Combe, in "Principles of Psychology" (1834) blamed swaddling and bandaging infants more than anything else, for deformities (Hayek 1954, 173).

"A cripple, deformed at birth, was exhibited as a kind of show in the hall of a benevolent nobleman. This spectacle was repeated night after night to impress the fashionable world of London that this unhappy wretch was produced by factory labor" (ibid. 178).

The mills suppposedly spread disease. Scrofula (TB of the lymph nodes) was common. Reformers blamed the mills for promoting it but the following is from a letter by Dr. E. Carbutt, physician to the Royal Manchester Infirmary, written to the Factory Commissioners: "Gentlemen...I wish to make a few observations...as to the great exaggeration of medical witnesses...on the subject of the diseases of the cotton factories. These gentlemen, hardly any of whom have ever had an opportunity of seeing persons employed in cotton factories, do almost universally attribute to factory labor, the production of scrofulous diseases. Now the fact is, that scrofula is almost unknown in cotton factories...To our surprise, the cotton factories are...a kind of means of cure" (Ure 1835, 376). "This is attributed to the dryness and warmth of the cotton factories and the lightness of the work" (ibid., 377).

Also: "During the prevalence of cholera at Stockport, the mill workers enjoyed a remarkable immunity due to the dry air...the cholera patients were almost all females employed in private dwellings" (ibid., 378).

While Engels blamed the "crowded and filthy conditions of the workers" for typhus epidemics, he also grudgingly conceded that it was not the established industrial hands who were the victims. "Dr. Southwood Smith, in the annual report of the London Fever Hospital for 1843 stated that... typhus raged in the damp dirty slums of East, North and South London. Many of the patients in the London hospital were migrants from the provinces who had endured dire privations both on their way to London and on their arrival in the capital. Unable to find work, they suffered from lack of food and had to sleep in the streets with insufficient clothing to cover them. It was in these circumstances that they caught fever" (Engels 1958, 112).

Also: "Mr. Harrison (is) Inspecting Surgeon appointed for the mills at Preston. There are 1656 employed under the age of 18. The average annual sickness of each child is not more than 4 days. I have not been a little surprised to find so little sickness which can be fairly attributed to mill work" (Ure 1835, 379).

Dr. Andrew Ure compared the medical testimony of the Sadler Committee to Molière's play, "Malade Imaginaire." He said, "One ingenious physician, when asked about the effects of night work on factory children, condemned it 'because Dr. Edwards of Paris found that if light is excluded from tadpoles they never become frogs'" (ibid., 374).

## FRIENDLY SOCIETIES: VOLUNTARY SOCIAL SECURITY

Twentieth century governments proclaim that their social security benefit programs, such as retirement funds, unemployment insurance, workers compensation and medical plans, are all State innovations. The assumption is that prior to these programs, workers' lives were filled with uncertainty, dependency and horror.

This is incorrect. Through "Friendly Societies," nineteenth century working families had a "safety net" long before governments became involved. Each member of these private sector benefit plans decided *when* to retire, the length of unemployment coverage, the depth of medical and life insurance coverage. Actuarial tables generally determined the fee. The enormous advantage of this system over today's schemes is that it did not tie a worker to a single job or depend on the stability of government.

In the mid-eighteenth century, as the Industrial Revolution hastened the growth of British towns, the Friendly Society system became well established. Sometimes they were called fraternal societies, mutual aid societies, or benefit clubs. Similar organizations developed in the United States in the nineteenth century.

The long-term success of the Friendlies reflects that they were much more than benefit institutions. Friendlies were voluntary self-help asssociations, organized by the members themselves. The workers regarded the Friendlies with great pride, as their own creation. More than just a means of support, they brought independence from the degradation of charity.

Friendlies served social, educational, and economic functions, bringing the idea of insurance and savings to those who might not have planned for the future. The social aspect of the Friendlies should not be underestimated. Their meetings included lectures, dramatic performances, and dances to both inform and entertain members.

Since members took turns at managing the Friendlies, the typical workingman developed executive skills that could prove valuable in his everyday employment.

Nineteenth century commercial insurance companies could not compete with the Friendlies, so they focused on business clients and the rich. Workers were suspicious of them because of their numerous failures and scandals. Besides, insurance rates were higher than those the Friendlies charged for comparable benefits. The reason was that Friendlies did not solicit. Thus, there were no salesmen and no commissions. Also, the member management worked on a volunteer or token salary basis (Basye 1919, 41-52).

Friendlies usually were formed by people with a common denominator, like the same occupation or same ethnic, geographic or religious background.

## TYPES OF FRIENDLY SOCIETIES

Unlike today's compulsory and standardized State-run plans, Friendlies provided dozens of benefit packages. Each person created their own plan. One could retire at 60 or even 50 or get unemployment or illness aid equal to one's own wages. All that was required was a high premium (Price 1803, 141-142).

Originally, Friendlies insured against "disability to work," with little distinction between accident or sickness. This also came to mean "infirmity," that is, insurance against old age. Most Friendlies paid for a doctor's services, burial expenses, annuities to widows, and educational expenses for orphans. They built old-age homes and sanitariums for members and their families. Even in their early stages, they offered unemployment benefits for those in "distressed circumstances" or "on travel in search of employment." The most common payouts were for maternity leave and retirement pensions (Baerneither 1891, 164).

## DIVIDING SOCIETIES

These were among the earliest British Friendlies, developing in the 1750s. After making payments for specified "events," (sickness, retirement, death, unemployment) the society would divide the balance of its fund among its members at the end of the year. The downside of this was the need to constantly recruit young people because these societies had no reserves, and the bulk of their claims tended to come from older members.

Still, their appeal was considerable. Each contributor received an annual return even when things were going well. The fees were uniform and easy to calculate. They used no actuarial tables (which were considered morbid by predicting the odds of sickness and death). The contributions were higher than other types of Friendlies, but the members got back a lump sum at the end of the year. Dividing societies combined insurance with the idea of savings; as such, they advanced loans to members.

A good example of a dividing Friendly was the Union Provident Sick Society. In 1880, its rules provided that no one would be admitted under age 16 or over 31. A 12-man executive committee was rotated among the society's members. Meetings were held "every quarter night." There was a small entrance fee and a small contribution every two weeks. Eighty percent went into the fund, 20 percent toward management. Benefits were roughly 25 to 33 percent of weekly wages for a year, and 15 to 20 percent for the remainder of the illness. For members over the age of 20, contributions and benefits were double. The surplus was divided each December, the members receiving shares in proportion to their contributions.

Five percent of the Union Provident's members were self-employed tradesmen or manufacturers who did not need the society's help. They had been workingmen when first admitted but still remained to show their moral commitment and to donate their managerial skills to the society.

Friendlies that did not divide gave higher benefits. One example was the Hitchen Friendly Institution. It provided benefits equal to full pay for a year to a member who was out of work due to illness, and half pay for the remainder of the ailment (ibid., 171-178).

## DEPOSIT SOCIETIES

An English clergyman, Reverend Samuel Best, originated this more sophisticated system. He introduced the concept of savings to early industrial workers. The deposit system connected the savings account with an insurance account so that the benefits for sickness or distress were derived partly from each. The member had a specific credit in the insurance fund based on his savings, but the claim ceased as soon as his own fund was exhausted. This promoted thrift by encouraging the member to add to his savings but not drain off the account.

If a person was healthy throughout his working life, when he retired he would have a large amount in his personal account. With much sickness and exhausted savings, the sickness or distress benefits ended but were replaced by "grace pay," which could be drawn for as long as benefits had been drawn. Grace pay related to the amount of savings.

The deposit system had major advantages over others. It did not use actuarial tables, which would force higher contributions on the elderly or sick, or exclude them from membership. Admission was without limitation (Beveridge 1948, 45-50).

## BURIAL SOCIETIES

This was the one area where commercial insurance companies competed successfully because the "event" (death) was easy to verify and actuarially predictable. For a long time burial societies were illegal because they "gambled on death" (ibid., 53-58).

## FACTORY SOCIETIES

There is a widespread belief that the nineteenth century factory owner provided no benefits for his workers. This 1891 report proves otherwise: "There is scarcely a single large establishment...which does not make provision for its employees, whether accident, sickness or burial. The management is in the hands of the workingmen, while the firm acts as treasurer, exercising some supervision, and represents a moral influence through its chief officers. Membership was supported by the firm. These subsidies gave substantial benefits for small contributors" (Baerneither 1891, 201-205).

Another study noted that "the mill owners have created a fund, applied to the encouragement of women to cease work for a sufficiently long time before and after the birth of their children to prevent injury to the constitutions of mother or infant" (Cross 1974, 75).

## BUILDING SOCIETIES

Building societies were workingmen's financial institutions. They loaned money to members for the purpose of buying a home. The "Terminating" type ceased existence when all the members had all bought a residence. The "Permanent" type had more characteristics of a contemporary bank.

These societies had a powerful influence, which still continues. Between 1918 and 1939, half of the homes built in England were purchased with the aid of building society funds (Beveridge 1948, 96-101).

## FRATERNAL SOCIETIES

Fraternals were more like life insurance companies in that they tended to focus on death benefits and pensions. Because of this, in the long run, they were more easily absorbed by the large commercial insurance organizations.    There    were dozens of variations of fraternals.  Those with branches (or lodges) were commonly called "affiliated" or "federated" orders, with divisions of power between the central administration and the regional branches.  Those without branches were referred to as "unitary" societies (Basye 1919, 122-132 and Beveridge 1948, 34-36).

## DOWNFALL OF FRIENDLIES

The Friendlies did not collapse financially, nor did they disappear because they failed to do their job for working people.  *They declined because of government action.*

British aristocrats feared the Friendlies because their huge contributor funds were viewed as a means for political subversion.  Over a two-century period, a steadily growing web of uniform State-mandated benefits first duplicated, then gradually absorbed the "dangerous" Friendlies.  Eventually, the National Insurance Act system largely replaced them.

In the United States congressional legislation slowly diffused the benefit and cost advantages that the Friendlies had over commercial insurance.  This led to their demise. That meant working people had far fewer benefit options (Beveridge 1948, 63-84 and Basye 1919, 113-122).

Throughout the capitalist world, the free institutions of working men were everywhere gradually brought under State control, and absorbed in the apparatus of the State.  The free workers of the nineteenth century have become the chained slaves of the twentieth century—and beyond.

# REFERENCES

Abbott, E. *Women in industry.* New York: D. Appleton & Co. 1910.

Aspin, C. *Lancashire, the first industrial society.* Rossendale, Lancashire: Helmshore Local History Society. 1969.

Baerneither, J.M. *English Associations of Workingmen.* London: Swansonnenerchein & Co. 1891.

Basye, W. *History and Operation of Fraternal Insurance.* Rochester: The Fraternal Monitor. 1919.

Beveridge, W.H. *Voluntary action.* New York: Macmillan & Co. 1948.

Cross, M., ed. *The workingman in the 19th century.* Toronto: Oxford University Press. 1974.

*Daily Mail and Express.* Toronto. October 7, 1897.

Engels, F. *The condition of the working class in England.* New York: Macmillan & Co. 1958.

Hayek, F., ed. *Capitalism and the historians.* Chicago: University of Chicago Press. 1954.

*Manchester Guardian,* May 1, 1844.

Price, R. *Observations on reversionary payments.* London: T. Caldwell & W. Davis. 1803.

Stearns, P. *The impact of the Industrial Revolution.* Englewood Cliffs: Prentice-Hall. 1972.

Ure, A. *Philosophy of manufactures.* London: C. Knight & Co. 1835.

# CHAPTER 3

# SAMUEL SMILES IS FROWNING: THE WORK ETHIC TODAY

*David Marsland*

This chapter offers a critical examination of British intellectuals'—particularly social scientists'—attitudes to work. Most of our intellectuals, themselves mainly in well-paid, protected work in teaching, research, or the media, treat Samuel Smiles and the core Victorian values of hard work and self-help which his writing enshrines as a real laugh. They hold the work ethic, on which the continuing economic prosperity of liberal democratic societies depends, in complete contempt. These negative attitudes powerfully influence and, if they go unchallenged by intellectuals with a different view, in the long run perhaps determine, general orientations to work in the population as a whole. This counter-Smilesian, anti-Thatcherite line, peddled actively in the media and the education system, is bound to weaken Britain's economic performance and thus to sabotage our freedom.

## WORK AND EMPLOYMENT

I examine here two sources of evidence about intellectuals' attitudes to work: first, the introductory teaching material of sociology—drawing on my book "Seeds of Bankruptcy" (Marsland 1988); second, an influential collection of papers on work called "On Work," edited by Professor Pahl of the University of Kent (Pahl 1988).

I preface these two main sections of the chapter with a brief account of some empirical evidence which seems to indicate that, however antithetical to the work ethic our intellectuals may be, the mass of British people remain nonetheless more sympathetic to Samuel Smiles. There is still time and scope to wipe the worried frown from his face.

### POPULAR ATTITUDES TO WORK

"Values and social change in Britain," edited by Mark Abrams and others and published by Macmillan in 1985, is a report of parts of a Europe-wide study of values. Its empirical methods were sound. Over 12,000 people, appropriately selected, were interviewed in ten countries. Consider Table 1.

It appears the British claim to take more pride in work than other Europeans—and far more than do Germans. They are quite well satisfied with their jobs, more so to a slight extent than other Europeans. They look forward to work significantly more than other Europeans. They are marginally less inclined than others to want work to play a smaller part in their lives, and the proportion who want less emphasis on work is modest. Moreover, if they had more free time without loss of pay, the British are more likely than others to look for additional paid work.

This all seems, granted the limitations of the research method which leaves scope for people to behave differently from the way they talk, quite encouraging. The British appear thoroughly positive about work themselves, and rather more positive than other Europeans.

**Table 1: Abrams et al, page 175**

| | Britain | W. Germany | 10 European Countries |
|---|---|---|---|
| | | (% or score) | |
| Takes a great deal of pride in own work | 79% | 15% | 35% |
| Job satifaction (scale 1-10) | 7.72 | 7.05 | 7.29 |
| Looks forward to work | 72% | 57% | 60% |
| Good if work played a smaller part in our lives | 26% | 30% | 33% |

**Table 2: Abrams et al, page 177**

| | Britain | W. Germany | 10 European Countries |
|---|---|---|---|
| Owners should run or appoint managers | 50% | 47% | 35% |
| Owners & employees should select managers | 37% | 37% | 41% |
| Employees should own and appoint managers | 7% | 7% | 10% |
| State should own & appoint | 2% | 2% | 4% |
| High level of confidence in major companies | 48% | 34% | 39% |
| Orders at work should be followed even when not fully agreeing | 49% | 28% | 32% |
| If two secretaries do the same job, it is fair to pay better performance higher | 65% | 64% | 59% |

Moreover, as Table 2 suggests, attitudes toward the organization of work are also positive. Overall, British attitudes are similar to those Europe-wide, with a rather greater inclination to support owner-power, an even slighter level of support for state power in industry, higher confidence in major companies, a stronger tendency to be well-disciplined, and a high level of support for meritocracy.

The author's comment is as follows (pg. 176):

> The British express relatively high satisfaction not only with their own work, but with the general business and industrial framework in which it is set. Half of them, compared to 35 percent across Europe, express outright support for capitalist ownership and management. Their confidence in major companies is above the European average...so is their readiness to carry out orders at work even if not first convinced they are justified. A large majority take a strong line on economic incentives: pay should be related to personal performance rather than simply to job level.

On top of all this, British confidence in trade unions is happily even lower than elsewhere—26 percent in Britain, 32 percent in Europe as a whole, and 36 percent in Germany. Moreover, 69 percent in Britain prefer freedom to equality, scarcely less among the low-skilled or the young, who might be expected to prefer equality.

Even in relation to these remarkably positive findings, the author typically manages to find a negative purchase. He would like the British to be more critical about work, more concerned about pay levels, more supportive of trade unions as "agents of change"! Here we are back with the anti-capitalist, post-industrial intelligentsia again. The people themselves, by contrast, are quite solid and sensible—and the same pattern of attitudes has been demonstrated again and again by similar research more recently.

Admittedly, there are grounds for concern by rigorous Smilesian criteria. A third of the working population supportive of employee-selected managers, even in conjunction with owners, might give one pause. A similar proportion averse to payment by performance is more worrying still—though it wouldn't be a bad figure among doctors or university teachers. Even more concerning is variation in work attitudes among groups defined by political orientation. For example, support for payment according to individual performance varies from as high as 73 percent on the right through the average of 65 percent, down as low as 41 percent on the far left. Similarly, support for owners running businesses and appointing managers falls from an average of 50 percent down to a meager 26 percent on the left.

Nonetheless, there appear to be no good grounds for believing that Samuel Smiles would be more than slightly disappointed with the work attitudes of most ordinary British people.

## INTELLECTUALS AGAINST THE PEOPLE: SOCIOLOGISTS' WORK DOCTRINES

It would be difficult to find a bigger contrast between popular and intellectual beliefs than the gulf between the work attitudes of the British population revealed in the European Values Study and the curious doctrines propagated by teachers of sociology. I draw my evidence about the latter from a study of "O," "A," and introductory degree level curricula and examination papers, and the thirty-six most commonly used textbooks, which I reported in "Seeds of Bankruptcy" (Marsland 1988).

Max Weber's *The Protestant Ethic and the Spirit of Capitalism* has been subject to extensive criticism ever since its publication in 1904-1905. Some of this criticism is certainly valid. Weber's analysis remains, nevertheless, one of the few genuine contributions by sociology to the advance of real knowledge. Its fundamental insight into the requisite institutional and psychological underpinnings of capitalism remains to this day incontestable.

What Weber enunciated—indeed celebrated—was the indispensable role in the development of capitalism of active and positive attitudes to work, and of values justifying such attitudes. Surely he was right. Among the prerequisites of the survival of liberal democratic society, none is more essential than systematic, enthusiastic commitment to conscientious, hard work on the part of at least a large proportion of the population.

Commitment to the work ethic presupposes, in its turn, a number of other characteristics in any society which intends to become or remain capitalist, and to avoid entrapment in feudalistic, authoritarian, socialist, or other forms of serfdom. Below, I examine five further work-related aspects of capitalism. Each of them has been increasingly subject to attack in recent decades. Sociologists, as evidenced by the teaching material I have examined, are in the front rank of anti-capitalist critique of work and the work ethic. Undermining work is one of the major effects of the arguments deployed routinely by sociologists in their prejudiced, negative treatment of business, freedom, and capitalism.

First, capitalism requires that a positive value be set on hard work for its own sake. If work becomes generally interpreted as merely instrumental, as nothing more than an unavoidable means of getting a livelihood, neither work commitment by the individual, nor positive attitudes to successful work by others can be ensured.

The persisting influence in Britain of pseudo-aristocratic attitudes, which construe work as banausic and not for "gentlemen," tends strongly in this direction. This is expressed through several distinct channels. For example, the older universities sometimes appear, even in the 1990s, to hold some kinds of work—in industry, in connection with technology, in sales and marketing—in contempt, and to regard work as a whole, at best as a regrettably unavoidable interference with more important pursuits. Again, the mass media and the world of entertainment are often guilty of creating the impression that luck and glamour matter more than talent and effort. And yet another example is provided by the increasingly influential (yet remarkably incoherent) concept of "the leisure society" or, as it is sometimes called, "post-industrial society."

These notions, which proffer a vision of "Brideshead for the people," as it were, serve to distract attention from work to play. They provide a convenient rationale for those whose purpose is to undermine commitment to work in Britain. High levels of unemployment offer wider opportunities to those who are enemies of the work ethic to argue for a shift in priorities from work to leisure, and for basic income to be provided "socially"—as a right of collective citizenship—rather than individually, in return for effort expended.

The material I have examined reveals sociologists as confirmed supporters of this anti-capitalist critique of work and of individual responsibility for self-reliance through work.

Second, positive valuation is required for the whole range of types and levels of work. If conscientious commitment to work is to be ensured in a free society—which denies itself resort to compulsion such as socialist societies routinely use to get difficult work done—there can be no caste distinctions in the work world which define some employment as suitable only for untouchables. Even if income and status differentials for different types of work are allowable, indeed required, there can be no class distinctions which brand some occupations as beyond the pale—otherwise the whole ideology of work which capitalism requires is liable to collapse.

I have already referred to the prejudices against industrial, technological, and commercial work which serve to distract many able young people away from lines of work which are more useful and productive into the older professions and the more gentlemanly world of high finance. Here, Britain loses out substantially, by comparison with the United States, Germany and Japan, where there is little trace of our fear of pollution by involvement in the market, in industrial production, and in sales.

Even worse is the growing prejudice against manual work of all sorts, which deflects many young people into futile clerical jobs as protection against the presumed insecurities, squalor, and lack of dignity spuriously associated with manual work. This prejudice is strongly encouraged by many school teachers and by other professionals involved in services for young people. The effect is to persuade them to prefer unemployment on the dole rather than accept hard and relatively low paid manual jobs.

It is peculiarly ironic for sociologists, of all people, to peddle contempt for manual work, as they regularly do in introductory course material. It is manifestly a form of class prejudice, which is allegedly sociologists' bête noire.

This attitude has found powerful support in the writings of sociologists and other social scientists about job satisfaction. Quite contrary to all the empirical evidence, which suggests remarkably positive attitudes to their own jobs by all sorts of workers—including those in so-called "unskilled" and "menial" roles—this literature speciously claims that most people don't enjoy their work and do it mainly for the money, from habit, or at best for the benefits of companionship. In fact, 80 percent and upward, according to most properly designed research studies, positively enjoy their work.

The material I have examined takes this wholly unjustifiable line consistently. It emphasizes, regardless of relevant evidence, the alienating effect of work. Little wonder if young people, influenced by sociological thinking (which permeates the media), are tempted into rank snobbishness, or reduced to hopelessness about their own prospects in the world of work.

In fact, according to Thierry and Iwema (Drenth et al. 1984), studies of work satisfaction internationally reveal that "the percentage of respondents reporting that they are satisfied is always high, and furthermore that this percentage has gradually increased.... In the last few years, 80-85 percent have reported that they are satisfied." A recent cross-European study states that "most Europeans in paid employment report high levels of satisfaction with their jobs" (Harding et al. 1986). The same study, based on a sample of over 12,000, found that job satisfaction is higher in Britain than in any other Western European countries except Denmark, Ireland and Holland. Students of sociology have these rather important facts carefully hidden from their view by their teachers.

Third, a successful capitalist society absolutely requires a generalized belief in opportunity. What this involves is faith that work openings cannot be significantly blocked by irrelevancies such as class, sex or ethnicity, and conviction that talent and effort will be rewarded by acknowledged success, including career progression, with the influence of mere time-serving or trade union norms effectively controlled. In short, some genuine approximation to meritocracy.

In this regard, sociological influence has been almost wholly pernicious. Except perhaps for the BBC and the quality newspapers, no one else has done so much to undermine belief in Britain as a society of opportunity open to talent and effort. For example, sociologists of education played a decisive role in the period since World War II in persuading our elites of imaginary weaknesses in the schools. They inaugurated changes in educational ideology and organization which have actually reduced opportunity, flexibility and social mobility.

Again, studies of stratification have persuaded many people, quite contrary to the facts, that Britain is a rigidly structured society, with privilege inequitably maintained in undeserving hands, and the poor and the weak denied all chance of progressing. And sociologists of work have for thirty years or more attacked the very concept of "career," and discouraged consistent effort at work success. All that is required, apparently, is for one to fix a "nice number," keep one's nose clean, and wait quietly for a pension!

The sociologists whose work I have examined (Peter Saunders, writing in Chapter 4 of this book, is a remarkable exception) largely share these prejudices. Scarcely any of them regard Britain as a free and open society, offering opportunities in the world of work for success and advancement. Most, indeed, would view this concept–which is an essential element in any coherent vision of Britain as a prosperous liberal-capitalist democracy—as hopelessly old-fashioned and unattractive. They are as antithetical to liberal individualism in the occupational sphere as in every other.

Fourth, successful capitalism requires the maintenance of a system of economic incentives which reward initiative, enterprise and effort, and penalize laziness and failure. It also needs commitment by the population at large, including the less successful and the less well paid, to the defending of this reward system.

Here, sociologists' influence has been peculiarly malign. For sociological writings, strongly reflected in the teaching material I have examined, urge with one voice the desirability of economic egalitarianism. They emphasize and exaggerate inconsistencies and inequities in economic rewards. They underestimate grossly the effects of successful work in improving the quality of life of those who work hard and efficiently at all sorts of levels in the occupational system. They consistently support social policies which require increased taxation and reduce financial rewards for hard work. They press for increased welfare provision despite its disincentive effects on the swelling numbers of welfare dependents. They underestimate the significance of economic incentives in the motivation of conscientious work. And they tend to support collectivist pressures from trade unions, professional associations, and big business for reduction in the scope for individual-to-individual differentials in wages and salaries (Marsland 1993).

Students of sociology need to learn about the economic realities of the work world. They should not be prejudiced by the egalitarian fancies of their teachers against understanding the essential role in free societies of economic rewards and incentives.

Fifth, and finally, it is essential that returns on work to the community as a whole should be recognized and celebrated. Here, sociologists make every effort to show that—even if a competitive system of economic rewards might conceivably and regrettably be justified on efficiency grounds—its narrow advantages in this respect are outweighed by moral considerations and by its negative social consequences, particularly alleged neglect of the public domain and community needs.

The material I have studied almost entirely ignores the dependence on the capitalist organization of work of:

- high GNP and therefore high standards of living nationally;
- the vast extent of welfare provision such as pensions and unemployment benefit, all of it paid for from the efforts of the working population;
- public provision of education, arts, and other cultural resources;
- and not least, the whole quality of life, culturally and environmentally, in Britain and other liberal democracies, which no other form of economic institutions has been able to rival.

The work values and occupational institutions I have described here are essential to liberal capitalism. Students of sociology need to have them explained fully and objectively, without the querulous negativism which characterizes typical sociological analyses. Unless this is done, we should not be surprised if they become skeptical about the sense and value of work itself, and prejudiced against the competitive organization of work which distinguishes capitalist from socialist, and democratic from authoritarian, societies.

By these five criteria, almost all the materials I examined fail to a greater or a lesser degree. The positive value of work, whether for individuals or for the community, goes signally unrecognized. The importance of positive attitudes to work goes unacknowledged. Lower status work is often treated as if it were too demeaning and unsatisfying to count as work at all. The intrinsic rewards of work are neglected. The focus of attention is on rigidities and inequalities in the occupational system rather than on the ample scope for advancement through work to other and better opportunities which the system uniquely provides. The positive role of economic differentials and incentives is consistently denied. In short, sociological treatment of work denies and undermines the meaning it simply has to have in a successful capitalist society.

The one apparent exception in the whole of the documentation I examined is provided by the Bergers (Berger and Berger 1975). Their book *Sociology: a biographical approach* seems to me to be, in general terms, more sensible and balanced in its handling of economic realities than most textbooks. Moreover, Peter Berger is the author of one of the minute number of books, *The capitalist revolution*, written by a sociologist, which positively celebrates capitalist civilization (1987).

Despite this, even their treatment of work incorporates many of the biases found in less careful and more dogmatic texts. Thus, they begin their analysis of work by saying (pg. 255) that: "Work has increasingly become a 'problem' for many individuals." This proposition is neither clear nor backed by any evidence. It is an expression of a commonplace romantic prejudice against work which the Bergers share with many sociologists, of the right and the left alike. It colors the whole of their analysis of work.

Admittedly, it does not, as in some textbooks, shape it entirely, for they are capable of sensible judgements, such as the following on the same page: "Technological production has progressively reduced the amount of time that most individuals spend at work." Yet overall they manage, nonetheless, to leave students with a vision of work as unrealistic, as idealistically romantic, as any I have found (pg. 256):

> All this has changed with modern industrialism. The vast division of labour brought about by the industrial revolution, which we have had occasion to refer to previously, has had as a consequence that most individuals participate in complex work processes which they cannot grasp in their totality. The classical case of such a process is the assembly line, where each individual worker only performs one minute operation within the total process. He is not concerned with, and need not understand, the steps in the process that lead up to his operation or the steps that follow it. His relationship to the work process, then is very fragmentary. Most important, he has no relationship—and may actually never see—the final product of his work. Whether or not this makes him unhappy, it almost inevitably leads to a situation in which he must question the meaning of what he is doing.

As they admit in a footnote, this is a generalized sociological version of Marx's theory of the "alienation of labor." They claim that "most non-Marxist sociologists today accept the basic insight, but trace the 'alienation' to technological production rather than to the forms of ownership of the means of production." It seems to me better characterized as a "blind-spot" than an "insight," whatever its provenance and credentials, and it is certainly not supported by the evidence (see above).

Whether in its original Marxist form or its liberal-socialist translation, it is only one way, and a peculiarly narrow and perverse way at that, of looking at work. At best, it has a very slender basis in empirical research, and none that is relevant is reported by the Bergers. Yet it controls and largely shapes the whole of their analysis of work. In consequence, it is vitiated by the pessimistic, romantic bias which distracts students' attention entirely from the more positive aspects of work, and disguises completely the crucial connections between work and the other fundamental economic dimensions of life in modern society.

Thus, even the most sensible and intelligent of sociologists are apparently caught up in prejudices about work which stand intractably in the way of realistic and objective analysis.

At the time when most of the material I have examined was being written, the escalation of unemployment in Britain was scarcely beginning. Now we find sociologists illogically lamenting the loss of types of work they dismissed earlier as scarcely fit for animals, and demanding subsidized protection for industries they condemned out of hand then as rank profiteers. Between these two periods, sociological misunderstanding of work has persisted. Almost none of the sociologists writing for and teaching young students seem to have any comprehension at all of the need for enterprising attitudes to work, and of a positive view of competition. One would imagine from their writings that work is a consumption-good like cake or baked beans, and moreover a commodity which is somehow in infinite supply.

Meanwhile, our competitors in Asia, in the USA and even elsewhere in Western Europe, take a quite different view of work, and reap the rewards of it in seizing British jobs away from us. What we need are sociologists who can provide teachers with more objective and more positive analyses of work, and teachers who can transmit an enthusiastic understanding of work—properly analyzed—to our young people.

## FASHIONABLE DISTRACTIONS

Pahl's book, a collection of edited readings called *On Work: Historical, Comparative, and Theoretical Perspectives,* was published in 1988 by Blackwell. Available as a very cheap paperback at £9.95 for 752 pages, it is obviously expected to have large sales. It is appearing widely on reading lists for degree and sub- degree work, and, more dangerously, for professional training of all sorts. The gatekeepers of sociological doctrine like it.

As the cover accurately claims, "*On Work* will be essential reading for students of sociology, history, and politics." Indeed, for the next five years, and with a new edition for the next ten, I would expect this book to become the main access to understanding of the nature of work for hundreds and thousands of students. It is destined to become the nineties equivalent of Bendix's classic "Work and Authority in Industry" (1956).

However, it differs from that book not only by reason of its broader scope and the changes in fashion which thirty years inevitably bring. In addition, it seems to me an odd, one-sided book which, in the light of its likely influence, we should be seriously concerned about; that is, supposing we believe that modes of understanding the nature of work matter somewhat more than trivially for the health of the culture and the economy in liberal democratic societies.

There seem to me to be six major weaknesses in the book. I comment briefly here on each of them, with two purposes. First, to "nail" important errors, as they seem to me, which are by no means unique to Pahl's book, but are becoming the stock in trade of current analyses of work in British social science. Second, to provide a basis for suggesting an alternative—more liberal and more positive—version of answers to issues in the analysis of work; issues which, however erroneous their treatment in *On Work* may be, are, each of them, important and need addressing seriously. Over and above this, I also deal with one further fundamental issue on which Pahl's analysis, which controverts the standard sociological line, seems to me correct—even if this in turn leads him into further errors. The seven issues are as follows:

- massive exaggeration of the significance of gender
- a promiscuously broad concept of work
- tendentiously one-sided interpretation of the historical development of work
- exaggeration of the extent of current change in work, and misconstrual of its nature
- a dangerously crucial logical role allowed to a bizarre essay on the philosophy of work by Sayers
- woolly pseudo-pluralism of the editorial material
- a valuable critique of Braverman spoiled by inadequate alternative theorizing

## EXAGGERATING GENDER

The single most remarkable feature of this likely influential book is the large amount of space given over to the gender issue. Yet Pahl himself is dissatisfied even with this. "The casual reader," he says (pg. 749), "might imagine that I have overemphasized the role of women's work, simply because nearly half of all the essays I have included are specifically about that topic. If anything I should perhaps have devoted more space to women's work and employment...."

Quite apart from the overpowering emphasis on women throughout the book, and the fact that the cover illustration is of a painting by Bonvin of a woman ironing, one whole section (Part 3) is given over entirely to the women issue. Called "Most of the World's Work," it occupies 120 pages, more than 15 percent of the whole book.

WORK AND EMPLOYMENT

Even if this represents a proper attempt at correction of earlier chauvinism in the analysis of work—and this is presumed rather than demonstrated—it is surely an excessive over-correction. It seems to have been determined less by objective analysis of the concepts, theories, and literature of work provided by economists, sociologists, psychologists, and other social scientists, than by the large proportion of sociology students constituted by women, and by the all-pervasive influence of radical feminism.

I cannot think that objective understanding of work is likely to be much assisted by a book in which the editor's introduction to Part 3 begins with the following sentence: "In retrospect it is astonishing that until the early 1970s most sociologists neglected any serious consideration of those who did most of the world's work." This proposition is simply not true, and the doctrinaire spirit in which it is presented is indicated pretty clearly by Pahl's footnoting it as follows:

"It is significant that it was not until 1980 that a United Nations report provided the following quotation now widely available printed as a postcard:

Women
constitute **half** the world's
population,
perform nearly **two-thirds**
of its work hours,
receive **one-tenth** of the world's income,
and own less than **one-hundredth**
of the world's property.

This statement has shifted from being dramatically challenging to being conventionally acceptable in a very short time."

That phrase "conventionally acceptable" seems to be a good deal more accurate than Pahl perhaps realizes. It may be irrelevant, untrue, misleading, and a serious distraction from the important task of examining the relations between women and work, but it has become regarded as self-evident gospel truth, and any challenge to it is treated as evidence of reactionary chauvinism if not of incipient fascism. This is surely no way to advance the analysis of work.

## STRETCHING THE CONCEPT OF WORK

Orthodox British analysis of work has hitherto certainly narrowed the concept excessively—particularly by focusing on employment to the extent of neglecting self-employment almost entirely, by giving exaggerated attention to operational work roles at the cost of ignoring management, and by insisting on emphasizing manual work—real work, as it were—while playing down the expanding non-manual, white-collar sector.

However, these errors are less influential in earlier British work, in American sociology, and in economic by contrast with sociological analysis. The situation is not in any case much helped, I think, by the general line adopted in *On Work*, which stretches the concept to the point of vacuity, while simultaneously maintaining the errors and omissions to which I have just referred.

This is apparent throughout the book, in the continuing thread of emphasis on women's work, and in particular in Part 4 of the book, "Forms of Work and Sources of Labour." This focuses on what Pahl claims are "the various forms of communal and informal work that are not conventionally considered in the contemporary analysis of work" (pg. 469).

Pahl's argument in the introduction to Part 4 and the selected readings which comprise it are an elaboration of the argument about "self- provisioning" promulgated in his earlier book "Divisions of Labour." This, it seems to me, trades on spurious criticisms of the family, on an absurdly exaggerated notion of the potential competence of the Welfare State, and on a serious and dangerous down-playing of the current and likely significance of straightforward paid work.

"Sociologists," he says (pg. 475) "have left the offices and factories of the formal economy to explore the changing pattern of all forms of work." Alas, it seems to me this heavy emphasis on "forms of work outside employment" is nothing more than a red-herring, and a dangerous influence on young people subjected to it—to whom employment (and self-employment) are presented as if, rather than being central and crucial to society and to the individual, they were entirely socially constructed, a mere product of passing capitalism, and due to be incorporated by some broader and truer concept of work in some better organized society of the near-future.

Mother to teenage son, lying in bed at ten o'clock in the morning: "Aren't you going to work, son?" Son replies:"I'm already working, Mum, honest. Ask a sociologist."

## INACCURATE HISTORY AT WORK

Part 1 of the book is called "Ways of Working in Former Times." The six essays it includes are, for the most part, interesting and valuable. Their overall effect, however, which is picked up and underlined by Pahl in his introduction to them, and at other points in the book, is to construct a simple, single line of development in the transformation of work, and to de-emphasize to the point of denial other aspects of the development of work which are at least as important.

The story Pahl tells, in his own words and through the selection of papers he has made, is purely and simply what he calls "the rise of the male breadwinner." Before capitalism and industrialism, we are supposed to believe that the main features of work were that it had no significant role for employment, and that men and women joined in the broad domain of work without significant differentiation between them. As a result of social transformation, what has happened that matters, according to Pahl, is the development of employment as the normative model of work, and the exclusion of women from this narrowed domain.

This seems to me both inaccurate and misleading. Employment work and specialization between the sexes in work as in other spheres are much older than capitalism or industrialism. Consider, for example, the accounts of work provided by Homer, Chaucer, and Shakespeare. They are indeed probably historically normal except in the very simplest types of society. Far from excluding women, the history of capitalism reveals a continuing gradual incorporation of women at increasingly high levels of the occupational system. Moreover, to suggest that this is the main line of development in the history of work is hugely misleading.

It encourages student readers to ignore other enormously important changes—above all, increasing efficiency, productivity, prosperity and standards of living. There is also radical improvement in the conditions and rewards of work; continuous upgrading of the skills and discretion required at all levels; transformation of the organizational structures and managerial systems of work; and, quite crucially, the development of freedom of choice in location and type of work.

All these positive developments disappear in Pahl's account, submerged almost entirely in a one-sided, misleading story about the inexorable rise of the male breadwinner, thrusting women back into the home as he appears, clutching his wrench in one hand and his employment contract in the other, above the historical horizon.

## EXAGGERATION AND MISCONSTRUAL OF CURRENT CHANGES IN THE WORLD OF WORK

I would not want to suggest that the nature and organization of work are not currently undergoing radical change, or that the pace of such change may not escalate over the next decade. Chapter 1 above and Chapter 10 below refute any such suggestion conclusively. However, the account provided by Pahl, particularly in Part 5 of the book "Disaggregated Capitalism, World Factories, New Technologies, New

Strategies, and New Contradictions" seems to me to exaggerate and miscontrue likely changes.

Pahl refers inter alia to "the current confusions about work," "diverse and challenging developments" in the world of work, work as "the key personal, social, and political issue of the remaining years of the twentieth century," "confusion and ambiguities about its meaning," "a restructured world of work," and "new ways and styles of getting the world's work done." Of course this is, in part, a sales speil for the book—why would people buy it if it hadn't a new story to tell? But in significant part he also means it, and it is an exaggeration.

For all the changes, there are also constancies—at least wherever liberal democracy is sustained or extended. All these are underplayed by Pahl's single-minded focus on change. For example: managerial authority; meritocracy; economic incentives; specialization; effort; individual rewards and satisfactions; societal outputs, economic and other; delayed gratification; the necessity for commitment; etc.

Moreover, the book's diagnosis of the character of changes in work is inaccurate, or at least one-sided. This largely follows from the book's one-sided history. If modern work history consists essentially of the rise of the male breadwinner, predicted change naturally and inevitably consists primarily in his decline. The main changes the book deals with are transformations in the relations between men, women and work, and reduction in the salience of employment compared with other forms of work.

On the latter he seems to me simply wrong. The whole population of the Third World is currently being recruited into employment. On the former, he exaggerates enormously—after all there are limits both in biology and in psychology to the extent to which women can replace men as breadwinners. Moreover, if the other major change he emphasizes—"the disaggregation of capitalism"—is, it seems, a latter-day, wish-fulfilling alternative version of the old

Marxist dream, it is neither explicitly argued anywhere in the book, nor plausible, nor even, except to socialists, desirable.

Pahl is quite rightly, in my view, skeptical about the concept of the "leisure society." But his own vision of the future of work seems at least as unlikely and even more unattractive morally, politically, or in economic terms. The major constancies of work remain central in the agenda of free societies for the foreseeable future. It is dangerous to persuade student readers otherwise.

## THE BOOK'S REAL STORY

Part 6 of the book, the last before a brief epilogue by Pahl himself, is called "Why Work?". It consists of two papers. The first is Ronco and Peattie's "Making Work." This is a relatively harmless (if not enormously useful) phenomenological, even softly ethnomethodological, exploration of how work is socially constructed, justified, and evaluated.

The second essay, by Sean Sayers and called "The Need to Work," is a different kind of thing altogether—although, placed to follow Ronco and Peattie, it trades rhetorically on their glib social constructionism. First published in "Radical Philosophy," the trade journal of British socialist wisdom, it is a downright Marxist critique of all the assumptions and principles which are essential to make work actually work in a free society. His revealing section headings are: Alienation; Women and work; Work and liberation; A false need?; Industry and human nature; The need for leisure; The politics of work; and finally, Socialism and work! He concludes—and Pahl's book concludes its collected contents—as follows:

> According to Lenin:
> The feudal organization of social labour rested on the discipline of the bludgeon, while the working people, robbed and tyrannised by a handful of landowners were utterly ignorant and downtrodden. The capitalist organisation of social labour rested on

the discipline of hunger.... The communist organis-
ation of social labour... rests... on the free and
conscious discipline of the working people themselves
who have thrown off the yoke both of the landowners
and the capitalist. This new discipline does not drop
from the skies, nor is it born from pious wishes; it
grows out of the material conditions of large-scale
capitalist production, and out of them alone.

Lenin was writing in 1920, when Russia was still
predominantly a peasant-based agricultural society.
His words must have seemed as utopian and as distant
from reality as Marx's.

If today, in our society, they still seem so it is for
different reasons. We live in a capitalist society, based
upon large-scale industry. For most people in our
society,work is in many respects an alienating and oppressive experience. The spur that drives them to it
may no longer be the threat of hunger as such, but
certainly the threat of serious material deprivation
plays its part. There is no question but that there are
material incentives to work, and yet the evidence, I
have been arguing, shows that work (at least of any but
the most repulsive and degrading sort) is also now felt
subjectively as a need. It may not yet be 'life's *prime
want*,' but it is a vital want, a need, nevertheless. So
far from being a utopian dream, Marx's vision is increasingly becoming a fact of modern psychology.
That is to say, the *subjective* conditions for a more
satisfactory and rational organization of the work of
society are developing here and now. What is lacking
is the *objective* framework of economic and social
relations, and the objective organization of work,
which would allow this need to be satisfied.

For all the to-ing and fro-ing of Pahl's own arguments, for
all of his equivocation on socialism, this is the unequivocal

concluding message he chooses to leave with his student readers. The same negative nonsense, the same old critical sabotage of work as I reported in "Seeds of Bankruptcy."

## PSEUDO-PLURALISM

On the other hand, it is enormously difficult to pin down Pahl himself in the editorial material in the book. In the modest sixty pages he allows himself, scattered between the several sections of the book, he offers almost no clear, definite propositions. All are hedged with apparently judicious ifs and buts and maybes. There are scarcely any clear, tight definitions even—criticisms of established definitions in abundance, but of coherent alternatives precious little sign.

The rhetorical effect of this is to leave the untutored reader imagining that the editorial line is open and pluralist. This cloaks the reality given by the selection and ordering of the readings, which is quite the opposite—an unambiguous, totally one-sided critique of normal, natural, and useful conceptions of work and its crucially positive role in the lives of men and women in free societies.

## WASTED REFUTATION OF BRAVERMAN

The one clear and, as it seems to me, valuable move in the whole book occurs in Part 2 on "Employers' Strategies and Workers' Strategies." Between them, his introduction and the readings provide a definite rejection and a coherent refutation of Braverman's sociologically fashionable thesis of "skill degradation."

Braverman's Marxist theorizing about the continuing, inevitable de-skilling of labor under advanced capitalism has dominated British industrial sociology for years—to the point of what I have called elsewhere "Bravermania." Skill degradation always was an implausible and remarkably silly notion, controverted by all the available empirical evidence, and maintained purely to shore up collapsing Marxist theories of work. It was brought in primarily to serve as a cloak for

Marxism's nakedness, once the immiserization thesis had been once and for all refuted by continuously improving general standards of living.

We should be grateful to Pahl and his authors at least for clearing Braverman out of the way definitively. Unfortunately, Pahl's alternatives are scarcely improvements. He concludes his analysis as follows (pg. 174):

> New divisions of labour are emerging that help to break down traditional lines of conflict and replace them with new ones. The arguments and issues that dominated the era of mass production and the collective workers are being replaced by new arguments and issues concerned with flexibility, fragmentation, deregulation and the distinctive strategies of management and workers.

This leaves him and those for whom he speaks with ample scope to continue sociologists' established presumption of the primacy in industry of conflict, the malevolence of management, the necessity for collective resistance by workers, and the happy coincidence of workers' "victories"—in the ongoing struggle against exploitative oppression—with social progress. We are thus back, by another route, to the usual unmitigated negativism about the whole world of work as it is organized in free societies.

## TOWARD A POSITIVE WORK CULTURE

Samuel Smiles' demand for hard work and self-help, and Max Weber's identification of the work ethic and the values which underlie it as essential foundations of liberal democracy remain entirely valid. Yet in Britain at least sociologists and other social scientists are sabotaging the work ethic systematically and routinely. The influence of their destructively negative attitudes toward work on hundreds and thousands of our young people (and through the media on millions) cannot be other than corrosive of the work culture as a whole in the long run.

Nor is this negativism restricted to the social sciences. It is common in the humanities, in the media, and not least in the world of the arts. For example, reviewing a nineteenth century servants' manual in the *Sunday Times* (August 20, 1989) the well-known novelist Paul Pickering sardonically concludes: "Thank God for the bad and unfaithful servant." We need a more accurate and a more positive understanding of work than our intellectuals are currently offering to support the positive work culture without which not only prosperity but freedom itself are at risk.

# REFERENCES

Abrams, M., et al. *Values and social change in Britain.* Macmillan. 1985.

Bendix, R., ed. *Work and authority in industry.* Wiley. 1956.

Berger, P.L. *The Capitalist Revolution.* Gower. 1987.

Berger, P.L. and Berger, B. *Sociology: a biographical approach.* Basic Books. 1975.

Braverman, H. *Labour and monopoly capitalism.* MRP. 1974.

Drenth, P.J.D., et al. *Work and organisational psychology.* Wiley. 1984.

Harding, S. et al. *Contrasting values in western Europe.* Macmillan. 1986.

Marsland, D. *Seeds of bankruptcy: sociological bias against business and freedom.* Claridge Press. 1988.

_____. "The wellsprings of motivation." *Modern Management,* vol. 4, no. 1. 1990.

_____. "Bureaucracy or enterprise? In defence of performance related payment." *Modern Management,* vol. 7, no. 4. 1993.

## WORK AND EMPLOYMENT

Pahl, R., ed. *On work: historical, comparative, and theoretical perspectives.* Basil Blackwell. 1988.

Smiles, S. *Self-help.* 1859.

Weber, M. *The Protestant ethic and the spirit of capitalism.* 1904-1905.

# CHAPTER 4

# SOCIAL MOBILITY AND MERITOCRACY

*Peter Saunders*

There is a conventional view of the class system in capitalist societies in general, and in Britain in particular. This holds that the class system is rigid and relatively closed. As Professor Bauer notes in relation to Britain, "It has become part of contemporary political folklore that a restrictive and divisive class system, almost a caste system, is the bane of this country. The system is supposed to be a major barrier to economic progress in Britain and also a significant source of justified social discontent" (1978, 1). According to this conventional view, those born into higher class positions tend to stay there, while those born into lower positions find it difficult to move up and out. Such social mobility as occurs is thought to be limited to short-range movement—for example, from skilled manual to routine white-collar employment.

This stereotype contrasts vividly with the ideal of a meritocratic system. In a meritocracy, the class into which you are born has no effect on the class location in which you end up. Those who occupy the top positions are those who have revealed the most talent, the strongest motivation and the greatest capacity for hard work. Bright and determined working class children enjoy just as good an opportunity to rise to the top as their counterparts from more advantaged backgrounds.

The conventional wisdom dismisses the claim to meritocracy advanced by ruling groups in countries like Britain and the United States as mere ideology. These countries claim to be meritocratic in order to legitimate their rigid class systems. If you can convince those at the bottom that wealth, power and prestige have been allocated according to talent and achievement, then you have gone a long way in securing the social order against internal challenge and dissent.

In this chapter, I seek to challenge this conventional view. I shall show that recent evidence on social mobility in Britain clearly supports a meritocratic interpretation of class recruitment. I shall also show, however, that mainstream sociology continues to reproduce the conventional view despite such evidence. It does this by resorting to what I see as a fallacious form of relativist reasoning.

## THE BRITISH CLASS STRUCTURE

Social class may be a key organizing concept of modern sociology but there is precious little agreement among sociologists over how to define or operationalize it. For the purposes of this paper I shall use John Goldthorpe's system of classification which is an attempt to apply Weber's theoretical principles to the analysis of contemporary class relations.

Goldthorpe allocates people to classes on the basis of two criteria. One is their *work situation*—the degree to which their job enables them to exercise authority or express autonomy. The other is their *market situation*—their ability to generate economic returns through the labor market. Putting the two together leads Goldthorpe to identify eleven social classes in Britain, although these are then collapsed into seven, five and eventually three principal clusters.

The distribution of people across these social classes is best gauged by the results of a recent national survey conducted by Gordon Marshall and his colleagues at the

University of Essex. According to their figures (reproduced below), around one-quarter of the population is found in the so-called 'service class' of professionals, administrators, managers and proprietors, while the rest of the population is divided evenly between the 'working class' and the various 'intermediate classes'.

---

### The British Class Structure

*The service class:*

| | | |
|---|---|---|
| Class I: | Higher prof. admin. managers & proprietors | 9% |
| Class II: | Lower prof. admin. managers & proprietors | 18% |

*Intermediate classes:*

| | | |
|---|---|---|
| Class III: | Routine non-manual & personal service workers | 20% |
| Class IV: | Small proprietors & farmers | 9% |
| Class V: | Lower grade technicians & supervisors | 8% |

*Working class:*

| | | |
|---|---|---|
| Class VI: | Skilled manual | 13% |
| Class VII: | Semi and unskilled manual & agricultural workers | 24% |

---

## HOW OPEN IS THIS SYSTEM?

When we consider the evidence on intergenerational movement across these seven social classes, we find a remarkable and apparently growing rate of social fluidity. Three major studies all reinforce the view of Britain as a relatively open class system.

The first was Goldthorpe's 1972 study of ten thousand males. He found (much to his surprise) that:

- only a quarter of the men in class I had been born into this class;

- over a quarter of men in class I had been born into the working class;
- sixteen percent of those born into the working class ended up in the service class;
- fifteen percent of those born into the service class ended up in the working class.

These are quite remarkable findings, not only because they reveal a high degree of movement across the whole range, but also because they show that more than one in seven of those born into the top positions end up at the bottom of the heap. The top social classes seem remarkably ill-adept at transmitting their privileges to the next generation.

Goldthorpe and Payne followed up this study in 1983. Following ten years of economic stagnation, they expected to find a worsening of social mobility rates. In fact, they found that the system had, if anything, become even more open! The percentage of working class children reaching the service class had increased by 50 percent (from 16% to 24%). There had also been an increase in the rate of downward mobility (the proportion of working class people who had themselves been born into that class had fallen from 60% to 53%). Despite the recession, opportunities for moving up (and falling down) the class hierarchy expanded during the 1970s.

The third and most recent study has been that by Marshall and his colleagues at Essex. This, too, confirms the pattern discovered by Goldthorpe. Indeed, the Essex team found that no fewer than *one-third* of those in the service class had started life in the working class.

## SAVING THE CONVENTIONAL WISDOM

Given data like these, it is difficult to see how anybody could continue to argue that Britain is anything other than a relatively open, fluid and meritocratic society. Yet argue they do. Indeed, the very researchers who brought us these findings have resolutely maintained that they do nothing to challenge the conventional view of Britain as a rigid class society in which the working class is highly disadvantaged. Goldthorpe, for example, insists, despite his evidence that "No significant reduction in class inequalities has in fact been achieved" (1980, 252). Similarly, Marshall and his co-authors confidently assert that "There have been no changes in social fluidity" (1988, 137).

Now sociologists, like journalists, have a vested interest in reporting bad news. As Richard Ogmundson perceptively observed some years ago, sociologists will generally attempt to transform good news into bad in order a) to maintain a basis for their continuing critique of the capitalist social order (for in Britain at least, most sociologists are also socialists by persuasion), and b) to maintain a flow of 'problems' to which they claim to have the solutions (or more usually, to which they assert the need for 'further research'). Evidence suggesting that Britain is a remarkably open society in which bright working class children can do well, while dull or lazy higher class children will do badly, is not the sort of evidence which most sociologists can bring themselves to accept. Rather, the response has been to reinterpret the evidence.

The way they have done this is by shifting the focus of attention from *absolute* to *relative* rates of social mobility. Thus, confronted by the findings reported above, both Goldthorpe and the Essex team shift the goal posts. The test of the openness of the class system is for them not whether large numbers of working class children end up in high positions, nor even whether children born into higher classes suffer downward mobility into the working class, but is whether children from the working class show an *equal* rate of movement into the service class as compared with children from higher classes.

The logic of this relativist approach lies in the fact that, as the capitalist economy has developed through this century, so the number of working class jobs has declined while the number of service class jobs has increased. Given this change in the occupational structure, it comes as no surprise to find working class people moving into professional and managerial positions since these jobs have expanded and have, therefore, inevitably recruited from the lower classes. The important point, however, is that while the changes of working class upward mobility have improved, so too have the opportunities for all other social classes. As the Essex team put it, "More 'room at the top' has not been accompanied by greater equality in the opportunities offered to get there" (1988, 138). Working class opportunities have expanded, but so too have the opportunities for all other social classes. In relative terms, therefore, nothing has changed. A child born into the working class is still seven times less likely to end up in the service class than is a child born into the service class.

This line of reasoning is used to justify the conclusion that the class system is still relatively rigid and closed. Absolute mobility rates have expanded but relative mobility rates are unchanged. The conventional view, therefore, still applies.

## THE FALLACY OF RELATIVIST INTERPRETATIONS

There are at least three reasons why this line of argument should be rejected as fallacious.

The first is that it ignores the evidence on *downward mobility*. Goldthorpe's evidence showed that 15 percent of those born into the service class wind up in the working class. But if the social order were really as closed and self-perpetuating as he and the Essex team would have us believe, such a high rate of failure in transmitting class privileges across the generations should not occur. Indeed, when we remember that the size of the service class has been expanding, it is really quite remarkable that more than one in seven service class children still end up slithering all the way down the system. Neither Goldthorpe nor Marshall and his colleagues offer an explanation for this. Such evidence is, however, entirely consistent with a meritocratic model according to which some children born into the higher positions lack the talent, motivation or dedication necessary to enter these positions and in consequence fail to emulate the achievement of their parents.

The second objection to the relativist interpretation is that it rests on the implicit assumption that the only change worth talking about is one where the working class gains *at the expense* of other strata in society. The development of capitalism has opened up new opportunities for members of *all* classes to aspire to well-paid and satisfying jobs. This phenomenon represents just one example of Hayek's metaphor of the 'moving column'—the idea that capitalism is an *unequal* but *dynamic* system in which a general rise in prosperity and life chances benefits all classes but does not erode the relative inequalities between them. Relative inequalities remain while absolute life chances constantly improve.

Goldthorpe and the Essex team dismiss this tendency as unimportant, however. What matters for them is not whether things are getting better for everyone, but whether those at the back of the column are catching up with those at the front. This perspective reflects their commitment to the classic socialist preoccupation with equality of outcomes as the sole criterion against which to measure the effects of social change. This is a view which applauds as progressive a stagnant economy in which the few plumb jobs available are equally open to children from all social backgrounds, but which remains highly critical of a growing economy in which far more working class children make it to the top but where class differences remain in patterns of recruitment.

The real objection to this kind of thinking is that it turns the very strength of capitalism into a vice rather than a virtue. Capitalism is inherently a) an unequal system, and b) a dynamic system. Relativist arguments ignore the generalized benefits which flow from the dynamism and focus solely on the inequality which (they fail to understand) is the necessary corollary of this dynamism. The fact that the number of service class jobs has increased (and hence that working class opportunities have increased) is taken as given—there is no recognition that this is the product of the very capitalist system which they seek to condemn. No matter how much capitalism improves the lot of all the people, relativist critics will forever complain that nothing is 'really' changing because some people still enjoy greater opportunities than others.

> Once upon a time, a giant and a dwarf clambered into a hot air balloon. The balloon's efficiency exceeded all expectations and most observers were delighted to see its continuing ascent toward the clouds. One group of disaffected sociologists remained resolutely unimpressed, however. When asked why, they triumphantly replied that the giant was still closer to the clouds than was the dwarf. Far better, they assured their bemused audience, to have dug a hole in the ground for the giant to stand in and never to have got involved with balloons in the first place.

The third reason for rejecting the relativist position is that it makes a tacit assumption which is never articulated, still less justified, to the effect that talent, motivation and the capacity for hard work are all equally distributed across all social classes in each generation. For Goldthorpe, as for Marshall and his colleagues, class of origin should bear *no relationship whatsoever* to class of final destination. If, say, 40 percent of the population is working class, then on this reasoning, 40 percent of doctors, managing directors and civil servants should have been recruited from the working class. Evidence that only one-quarter in fact came out of the working class is then taken as evidence of class bias in the system.

Obviously, this argument only makes sense if we assume that ability and motivation are randomly distributed across classes. This is precisely what the relativist argument does assume: "The presumption must be," says Goldthorpe "that to a substantial extent [class inequalities] do reflect inequalities of opportunity that are rooted in the class structure, and are not simply the outcome of the differential take-up of opportunities by individuals with differing genetic, moral or other endowments" (1980, 252).

But why *must* we presume this? Goldthorpe never provides us with a justification for this crucial presumption. In fact, it is a presumption which can and must be challenged.

## SOCIAL INEQUALITIES AND NATURAL INEQUALITIES

Traditional sociology never had any problem in accepting that individuals in society are differentially endowed with biological and psychological capacities. In *Division of Labour in Society*, Emile Durkheim looked forward to a time when social inequalities would come to mirror natural inequalities—that is, a society where no social barriers exist to prevent each individual from attaining that role in society for which he or she is capable. Durkheim was in this sense an early meritocrat, not so much on ethical grounds as by his belief that this was the only way to resolve the social pathologies of his time.

Modern sociology, however, is embarrassed by talk of natural differences between people and prefers to ignore or even deny their existence. Such is the case with the relativist interpretations of social mobility rates. Goldthorpe and the Essex team necessarily rule out as inconceivable a) the existence of natural differences in talents and abilities, and b) the process of genetic transmission of individual capacities across generations. This is because, if they were to accept the existence of natural endowments, their entire critique of British society would be unsustainable.

That there is a biological (as well as cultural) basis to human behavior is surely uncontestable. With training and much encouragement, I can learn to run faster or solve more complex mathematical problems, but I will never be able to run 100 meters in under 10 seconds, nor will I ever be able to fathom the complexities of modern nuclear physics. As A.H. Halsey (a leading figure in Britain's left sociological establishment) has recognized, "*All* characteristics are *both* acquired *and* genetic. Genotypes determine potentialities. Environment determines which or how much of these potentialities should be realized in living human beings" (1977, 2).

It is now equally uncontestable that genetic capacities are transmitted in complex combinations across generations. This is as true for behavioral as for physical characteristics (see Dawkins 1976, 65-66). This is not to say that any one set of intelligent or diligent parents will produce naturally intelligent or diligent offspring, anymore than blue eyes or a tendency to baldness in middle age will necessarily be transmitted directly from parent to child. But it is to recognize that *on average* there will be a tendency for more intelligent parents to produce more intelligent children, and vice versa. There is considerable dispute—for example, in the long controversy over measured IQ scores—regarding the relative significance of environment and heredity, but few serious observers would claim that IQ or any other indicator of character and capacity is *wholly and entirely* a product of cultural factors.

Now, given the existence of a) some genetic differences in behavioral capacities, and b) some genetic transmission across generations, what should we expect a meritocratic society to look like as regards rates of social mobility?

Clearly we should *not* expect to find equal representation of all class backgrounds across all occupational groups. This is because, under conditions of real meritocracy, *classes will already have been sorted by talent, ability, and so forth, in the preceding generation, and these differential capacities will then be reproduced to some extent in the generation which follows.* It is unrealistic to insist upon proportional recruitment from all classes unless a) you are willing to deny the existence of any natural differences between people, or b) you are willing to deny any degree of genetic transmission across generations. As we have seen, both conditions are unrealistic.

So if (using the Essex team's figures) 37 percent of the population is born into the working class, what proportion of those occupying top jobs should we expect to find coming from working class backgrounds if the society were, to all intents and purposes, operating on meritocratic principles?

Clearly the answer must be something less than 37 percent. If we found that something over a quarter of these people came originally from the working class, we should probably conclude that the society was highly meritocratic and was placing few obstacles in the way of talented individuals from the lower social strata. This, of course, is exactly what Goldthorpe and the Essex team did find!

Taking this together with the crucial evidence on downward mobility—the fact that 15 percent of the sons of the service class ended up in the working class—our conclusion must surely be that modern Britain is a case of a remarkably open class system in which a) most talented children who work hard end up in top positions, and b) children of middle class parents who are not very talented or not very hard working are quite likely to end up in relatively lowly positions despite their initial apparent social advantages.

This is not to deny that there are social barriers to advancement in this society. The very highest echelons of the traditional upper class can usually manage to preserve their privileges down the generations and there are undoubtedly specific obstacles encountered by women when compared with men and with racial minorities when compared with whites. It is, however, to insist that the familiar sociological orthodoxy is wrong and should be abandoned. Britain is not a pure meritocracy—no society ever could be. But the class system is relatively open and fluid, and contemporary evidence cannot sustain the myth of a closed social order.

## CONCLUDING COMMENT

Theorists of market capitalism have long argued that a market society will tend to be indifferent to social background. It is in the interests of employers to hire the most capable workers and of consumers to purchase the best quality goods at the lowest available price. Employers who hire only people with cut-glass accents, or consumers who purchase only from those with the right school tie, will in the end disadvantage themselves relative to other more rational actors in the marketplace. This chapter reinforces such theoretical arguments with empirical evidence, for we have seen that, to a large extent, recruitment to the best paid and most responsible positions in Britain is governed primarily not by class background but by individual ability and motivation. The one cause for complaint is that most sociologists seem so loathe to come to terms with this fact.

## REFERENCES

Bauer, P. *Class on the Brain.* London: Centre for Policy Studies. 1978.

Dawkins, R. *The Selfish Gene.* Oxford University Press. 1976.

Durkheim, E. *The Division of Labour in Society.* Collier-Macmillan. 1933.

Goldthorpe, J. *Social Mobility and Class Structure in Modern Britain.* Clarendon Press. 1980.

Goldthorpe, J. and Payne, C. Trends in inter-generational class mobility in England and Wales 1972-1983. *Sociology,* vol. 20, 1-24. 1986.

Halsey, A. *Heredity and Environment.* Methuen. 1977.

Hayek, F. *The Constitution of Liberty.* Routledge & Kegan Paul. 1960.

Marshall, G., Newby, H., Rose, D. and Vogler, C. *Social Class in Modern Britain.* Hutchinson. 1983.

Ogmundson, R. "Good News and Canadian Sociology." *Canadian Journal of Sociology,* vol. 7, 73-78. 1982.

# CHAPTER 5

# THE UNDERCLASS RE-VISITED: CAUSES AND SOLUTIONS

*Ralph Segalman*

Current thinking on welfare policy in the United States, as reported by Mead (1988), has undergone a number of changes. A more conservative approach seems to have been accepted by most policymakers and scholars, aside from those representing the political extremes. These concepts support workfare, greater freedom for state and local experimentation with welfare, and increased effort to secure parental support. The current debate focuses on issues of how much the federal government should support childcare while mothers are in school, training, or employment.

The earlier assumptions that all the poor were alike and that the poor were no different from the mainstream have been shattered by evidence of a long-term welfare class (Wrong, 1988 reviewing Moynihan). Thus, the belief that suitable jobs were not available for the poor has proven no longer credible in light of the fact that millions of immigrants, many of them marginally skilled, have found employment. The new policy in the United States challenges the legalistic approach based on claims of the poor that they are entitled to welfare regardless of their behavior. In its place, the new thinking stresses the importance of personal responsibility for 1) preparing oneself for employment and 2) providing the proper environment for educating one's children for life in the mainstream.

There are still some scholars who continue to resist the open recognition of the "underclass." Sheldon Danziger (1989) reviews a series of scholars who seek to explain away any definition of an underclass which places responsibility for the condition of the poor on the poor and on their chosen life patterns. They reject any indications that the life patterns which the persistent poor follow include a wide range of social pathologies, self-defeating behaviors, anti-social activities and the avoidance of human capital accumulation in the ghetto family. These are all choices made either unconsciously or consciously by the chronic poor which distinguish them from others in the society.

The definitions of the underclass proposed by Danziger and his associates seek to utilize parameters of poverty examination which are either so broad as to be unmeasurable or so narrow as to prove the non-existence of the phenomenon. More realistic parameters would identify the underclass family and its members, include multi-problem families with inadequate socialization of children, and behaviors which result in unemployability for jobs which would reasonably support a family. The families which are chronically unable to support themselves, chronically in difficulties with the law, and chronically unable to participate in mainstream processes might easily be identified by data already available to public authorities.

Two major structural changes in the nature of life of the residual poor have particularly worked as a brake on their contemporary social and economic progress. The first is the decline in the availability of unskilled employment and the increased educational and vocational requirements for service industries and jobs in high-tech fields. The second is the impact of desegregation in enabling successful Blacks and Hispanics to move out of the ghetto: many of those who remain are the least able to extricate themselves from dependency and other social ills. What remains is, in many ways, an almost classic case of what Oscar Lewis described as the culture of poverty which is, in part, reinforced by economic conditions as well as by a set of norms, values and beliefs that separate this population from life in the mainstream. In the United States, the interaction of a particular variety of public assistance, with the other factors already listed, creates a seemingly intractable series of syndromic problems. In the United Kingdom, the interaction between a broad range, in great part "socially conferred" social security system, immigration program and other related factors, has created a phenomenon sometimes described as "Brits at the bottom."

In addition to legislative and court imposed barriers, in the United States a major obstacle to welfare reform is the culture of the residual welfare clientele. The new view of welfare and the welfare clientele no longer sees poverty in America as a phenomenon that has resulted from a structural weakness in American society. Instead, this new view sees American residual poverty, in large measure, as deriving from a unique version of the culture of poverty in which the interaction of the American welfare system and the traditional dynamics associated with welfare dependency provide a transgenerational effect. The studies of Sheehan, Forman, Auletta, Murray, Segalman and Basu, Sandberg, and others have documented the existence of this new variety of culture or welfare poverty.

Oscar Lewis studied cultures in different sectors of the Third World (or almost Third World). Out of this work came his concept of the culture of poverty. Lewis argued that many of the residual poor live in an all-encompassing and self-reinforcing condition (1968, 4-18). It is self- perpetuating (1966, 19-25). He has listed some of the basic sociocultural traits of this level of poverty: 1) inability to plan for the future; 2) to seek immediate gratification; 3) an "oral" personality structure with weak impulse control; 4) an expressive lifestyle; 5) to value acting out more than thinking through a problem; 6) to self-expression more than self-constraint; 7) to pleasure more than productivity; 8) to spend more than save; and 9) to personal loyalty more than justice (1968, 29, 58).

The American version of the Culture of Poverty is somewhat different. American welfare, until the 1960s, served as a temporary expedient for families who had suffered social, economic or medical catastrophes, but these families were, in the main, equipped with employment skills and other human capital which made a return into mainstream life possible. In a 1935 State of the Union speech, President Franklin D. Roosevelt, the symbol of American liberalism, expressed the belief that continued aid was "a narcotic, a subtle destroyer of the human spirit, ...fundamentally destructive to the national fibre." By the 1960s, the nature of the welfare population was in the process of dramatically changing. While those on the welfare rolls were only temporarily receiving public assistance, there was an alarming increase in the numbers of families for whom welfare became a permanent way of life. Increased forms of benefits, especially medical assistance and food stamps, and the diminishment of social stigma for welfare, caused welfare to become an increasingly attractive alternative. Supplementary Security Income for the needy aged and physically or psychologically disabled became available for women who were no longer childbearing in the Aid to Families with Dependent Children (AFDC) population.

This program has exacted a heavy price on these families. Because this program was originally intended to help widows and helpless divorced and deserted women, families with healthy husbands were not eligible. As a result of this policy, many of these families now practiced "fiscal abandonment," that is, the husband actually lived at home but was reported as having deserted. Such a pattern is bound to leave a psychological mark. In other families, when the wives realized that by being without a husband they could receive AFDC money, the husbands found themselves less welcome and with diminished authority. These men were no longer treated as partners in the family and were not consulted on major family decisions. Many of them moved out of one family as husband and into another as temporary, unreported boyfriend. Now that AFDC has become generally available, along with food stamps and Medicaid, these financial supports have become more dependable providers for the family than were husbands with marginal, episodic employment. And the wife now had full control over the family and the funds.

In the case of young people, new families were not formed, and pregnant girls and young women went on welfare, while young adult males remained unmarried, unemployed and "on the street." The motivation for "settling down" no longer existed for the welfare men. The insidious, debilitating effect of this kind of assured but limited income on the family is made clearly evident by the married families' income maintenance study of the 1970s. This experimental program provided a guaranteed minimum income for thousands of families in Denver and Seattle. The results were startling. Even for families not previously on welfare, there was a sharp increase in family breakup (Albrecht 1979 and Popenoe 1988).

There may have been initial stigma for families which accepted welfare, but in time, as those who did not accept welfare moved away or as their children left the inner city for something better, a distinct welfare culture emerged in the central city. Those who accepted the welfare label and its stigma became increasingly isolated from the world of work, education, and upward mobility. A distinctive pattern of living on welfare soon emerged. The matriarchal family pattern, already endemic among some of the poor, became the mode. The kinship network consisted almost exclusively of women. This was not only because the husbands had left the household, but because the children in the family had different fathers (and little or no contact with many of their fathers). The only stable and available relatives were mothers and other women, most on welfare.

The usual or expected rites of passage for children into adulthood in the past had been high school graduation and employment. For this new group of children in welfare families, welfare had made education and preparation for employment far less relevant for their future. The new rite for many girls was pregnancy and unmarried motherhood. For boys, the symbol of manhood was now membership in the street-corner society. Full membership in this male society was not complete without fathering a child out of wedlock and establishing a series of transitory live-in relationships with little or no male economic or parental obligations. For many AFDC families, especially those where succeeding generations also established welfare families, childrearing was chaotic, inconsistent and ineffective. For welfare-dependent children, much of their preparation for adult life was learned from their peers on the streets.

Another significant development in the AFDC family was the change in expectations for their future. In the earlier AFDC population, the widowed, divorced, or separated woman tried to carefully plan her life and that of her children so that they would eventually become self-sufficient and free of charity. The new family viewed AFDC as a permanent, reliable source of support—one to which they were entitled—and which, realistically, required of them minimal economic planning and no effort.

For those women who were marginally removed from poverty or for many who came from middle class backgrounds, the presence of AFDC encouraged the use of alternatives that were often not in their best interest or that of the society. For example, adolescent girls (expressing the common rebellion against parents) allowed themselves to become pregnant and bear children, consciously aware that the biological father would play no further part in the raising of the children. They could do this mainly because of the availability of government funds. Even some middle class girls joined this population. They could minimize their connection with their parents—and did not have to consult with them regarding this pregnancy—and its implications for their future. Once on AFDC, many of these women became part of the dependent welfare population.

The belief that welfare was an acceptable way of life was mutually reinforced by recipients living in the same neighborhoods. This had the obvious effect of reducing the social stigma that earlier had influenced decisions of whether to accept welfare and whether or not to find ways to move off welfare. This also increased the social distance of these families from the rest of society. A body of updated welfare lore was passed on from family to family on how to get the most benefits and how to avoid the welfare audit process. The terms of AFDC eligibility precluded the presence of an employed father or mother, except where such employment is unreported and secret.

Still another attitudinal factor influencing the acceptability of welfare emanated from the urban ghetto itself. In such an atmosphere the residual poor were socially isolated from the mainstream society. This mainstream or productive society, making up the majority of the population, is strongly oriented to the "norm of reciprocity," that value system which believes in and adheres to the view that "one must give something to get something." This view is inculcated in the children of the general population, along with other values necessary to survive in the mainstream. The segregated nature of urban neighborhoods, schools, churches and other scenes of interaction also prevent the welfare-dependent from "rubbing elbows" with non-welfare families which are imbued with the values necessary to enter and maintain oneself in the general society. Most of those in the welfare population who retained the primary value of planning ahead, or protecting oneself against the future by savings and insurance, and the equally important value of preparing oneself for future self-support, somehow left the ghetto, especially as more attractive environments were now available to them elsewhere.

Many of those who remained, looked upon welfare as the way of life. In her book *A Welfare Mother*, Susan Sheehan reported her welfare mother as saying that she moved on to welfare because it was the best deal going, and if it were not available she would look for something else. But her daughter with a baby, now the second generation on AFDC, looked upon welfare as the *only* way of subsistence.

The pervasive and relatively easy availability of AFDC had an additional unintended but tragic consequence. It made mutual aid of the extended family appear less necessary; and it removed the incentive for local, private philanthropy to work for the rehabilitation of needy families. Further, it destroyed the rationale for the neighborly aid which had been the foundation of community cohesion.

Sheehan presents us with a description of some of the results of the adaptive process of residual welfare clients to the welfare "life space." These include a matriarchal pattern of family structure (because the husband's place in the family has been effectively supplanted by an impersonal, undemanding, consistently providing complex of faceless government agencies). Another condition of the residual welfare family is a multiplicity of children, perhaps not spurred on by the additional grant for each child as much as from the attractiveness of motherhood to the residual welfare mother, whose only productive outlet is biological. Klausner, in his study of "Young Love in Impoverished Families," indicates that for the residual welfare mother, who is often less capable of a relationship of personal adult social intimacy, especially with the opposite sex, "love" is primarily a response to being a mother (pp. 17-18). When the family ties do not hold well and where the wider family provides no stabilizing context, there follow problems, conflicts, adultery, drugs, physical

*100*

abuse, quarreling and termination of relations which is then repeated with another male partner without any sense of responsibility, and the government takes over the family's economic problems.

In her examination of teenage pregnancy, which is a sizable contributor to the growing population of residual welfare-dependent families, Janet Bode in *Kids Having Kids: The Unwed Teen-Age Parent* indicates that most unmarried motherhood comes to girls who have few or no occupational or social skills and that failure in academic and career preparation pursuits is a usual precursor of unwed pregnancy. Cherlin, in his *Labor Department Study,* indicates a major contributor to the culture of poverty, American style. He describes the correlation between the liberalization of AFDC requirements and the increased trend toward divorce and the altering of the traditional family structure toward female one-parent families. B. Frank Brown, in the study of "The School Needs of Children from One Parent Families" by the National Association of Elementary School Principals, reports that nearly half of American children born in 1980 (and presumably in subsequent years) will live "a considerable time" with only one parent and that a sizable proportion of these children will be beset with problems of low academic achievement, truancy, absenteeism, discipline problems, school suspension and academic failure. He indicated that many of these are welfare families. Thus, we can see the process of academic failure, personal and social failure interacting with adolescent parenting and welfare dependency as an intergenerational syndrome. This, in turn, is accompanied by female single motherhood and parenting, adolescent (and adult) unemployment, and all the social pathologies which accompany an idle street-corner male population.

Sheehan also reports only a tenuous relationship between the welfare family and the community religious organizations, school, community centers, youth services organizations, and employment placement and training programs. Similarly, she found little or no contact between the welfare family and the extended family. Apparently, the welfare system and its ready and regular availability has also displaced these institutions just as it has supplanted the husband in the family. These findings of institutional, community and extended family distancing are reflected in other welfare family studies, including those of Auletta and Sharff.

The view of life as seen by the mother in the family described by Sheehan was one devoid of aspirations or plans for herself and her children to raise them out of poverty. It must be noted that unlike the poor of previous times in American life and unlike many contemporary immigrant poor, the Sheehan welfare mother is not forced to plan ahead for herself or her family. In a sense, the viewpoint of the Sheehan welfare mother is almost identical to the description given by Edward Banfield in 1968 when he indicated that the underclass problems are "at bottom a single problem, the existence of an outlook and style of life that attaches no value to work, sacrifice, self- improvement or service to family, friends or community."

The life disorganization which occurs in Sheehan's *A Welfare Mother*, which derives from her present-oriented dependency on welfare, also has its effect on her family's home conditions and childrearing. Her childrearing orientation lacks authority, in part because she does not have the support of a co-parent or husband and in part because planlessness is a mother to fatalism—she sees no cause and effect process in her life and so does not know how to become a credible parent. Her control of the children is usually primarily physical and episodic in nature. The option of physical control is lost to her as soon as the children become larger than she is or can run faster than she can. Her present-oriented planless life pattern results in much impulsive behavior on her part, whether it relates to child control or family expenditures. Thus, the consistent availability and relatively substantial nature of welfare and its related benefits leads the residual welfare client into a life pattern which insures an ineffective pattern of child socialization. What does the welfare client do with herself and her time? According to Sheehan, she spends much of her efforts and activities in planless confusion, a pattern similar to Parkinson's elderly lady, who spends her day seeking to get a letter written but can't find what she's done with the address, pen, paper, envelopes and stamps, and when she does gather these items, she's forgotten what she planned to say.

The behavioral patterns of the mother in the Sheehan and Sharff studies probably serves as a role model to her children in their early years, which instills in them a set of life values and behavior which are not directed toward their escape from welfare dependency and its related urban ghetto life. When her control proves ineffective, her children then have to seek their role models in their peer groups, which, in the case of many of the males, amounts to socialization into gang life. Similarly, in the case of many of the girls, if they remain at home, they are bound into the social life of the girls of the neighborhood whose culture is strongly influenced by the attraction of adult life achievable only by becoming pregnant. Even if she remains in school, she sees many of her friends and peers moving into their own apartments with their babies, on welfare and dropping out of school. The baby is often seen as a solution to loneliness and to having nothing of her own. Often the welfare mother supports the welfare-dependent role for her daughter or the gang membership (family protective role) of the sons as in the Sharff welfare families study. Thus, the rearing of these children leads to a perpetuation of the family's intergenerational welfare-dependency and to a continued social chasm between the family and the productive social mainstream. It also insures that the children will continue to create families devoid of effective husbands and fathers and employed persons.

The American version of the culture of poverty is unique in that it is not the direct result of the level of poverty experienced by Third World populations. In fact, the income level of most of the population classed as poor would be considered to indicate affluence in many parts of the world. In our search for a solution to American welfare dependence, we must be concerned with how to undo those aspects of the welfare system which are part of the problem.

The welfare problem, however, also reflects the larger problems facing America's society. In the past, as many social thinkers have noted, the intact family has served as the primary vehicle of socialization, preparation and support for family members, and especially the children. As Nisbet described it, the family was a key "buffer institution" which served as a mediator and source of strength for the individual, standing between the individual and the larger society. The family also functioned to motivate and shape the individual to become a competent and accepted member of the larger society. While the weakening of the importance of the family has been apparent in the last half-century, it has been particularly undermined by the new views of marriage which became pervasive in the American culture beginning in the 1960s. It is most clearly illustrated by the legal changes which came about as people revised their views of the duties and obligations of marriage and parenting (formal and otherwise). In the 1960s, under the new laws, divorce is seen as a "no fault" issue, without blame on either partner for the failure of a marriage. Thus, if either partner in a marriage felt some discomfort in the relationship, even if children were involved, divorce, rather than working out the problem, would be the appropriate action. In past eras, families would avoid divorce even to the point of a condition which was frequently described by family counselors as "holy deadlock." Now the fashion among young parents is at the other extreme, in that the resort to divorce comes sooner and more frequently and "holy deadldock" is a rarity.

With this shift in what was acceptable or desirable, came a huge increase in divorce in the urban areas. Husbands seldom sought or gained custody of the children; and, in addition, women and children without a husband/partner became a more common model of the family. By 1983, almost half the children of America spent some part of their minor years (until age 18) in a single-parent family.

The consequence of the trend toward female-headed, single-parent families, whether caused by divorce, desertion or by the childbearing by unwed women, is dramatically illustrated by the recently published research of McLanahan (1988), who found that

> living with a single mother at age 16 increases a daughter's risk of becoming a household head (on her own and often on welfare) by 72 percent for whites and 100 percent for blacks....a daughter living in a single-parent household is far more likely (127 percent more likely among whites, 164 percent among blacks) to receive welfare benefits as an adult compared to daughters from two-parent families.

In the process by which the steady husband-father was converted into what was frequently called a "Disneyland Father," many fathers were permitted to see their children only for a few hours a week. Severe strains were more often the pattern of divorced parent relationships, and the issues of visitation rights, quality of child socialization, child support and division of family assets were frequently so drawn out as to make the divorce process a "forever" experience. Under these circumstances, as ex-husbands were pressed for increased child support or property division, or pressed for payment of court-ordered support, they would respond with counter-actions against their ex- wives. Ex-wives would respond by resisting or blocking child visitation arrangements, and ex-husbands would hold back on child support payments as a quid-pro-quo item. In time, many of these situations deteriorated to the point that the husband would disappear both physically as well as an economic support to the family.

Finally, the family would have to apply for welfare aid. If the woman in the family had an adequate schooling and vocational background, the AFDC aid would cease after the children were old enough for school and after the woman would become employed. If, however, the woman had inadequate preparation for employment and if welfare and its accompanying benefits amounted to more than the woman's potential "take-home" pay at the entry level job, then the more likely result would be acceptance of continual welfare to the point of welfarization of the family and that of the children's families.

Thus, in the United States, we have a growing population of female-headed families, many in their second generation of dependency, and with little probability of escape from the underclass syndrome. Many of these families live in geographical areas which are beset by the social pathologies of rampant juvenile delinquency, drug addiction and distribution, crime, gang warfare, child abuse, sexual promiscuity, prostitution, ineffective schools, family disruption, and unemployability, as well as all the externally related problems of unemployment, low social class status, unmet health needs, destroyed communities, and others. The underclass interacts with its ghetto surroundings in a symbiotic way. The dependent family is both a victim and a supply source of ghetto activity, in that the participants in ghetto crime and drug activities are frequently the graduates of the welfare family (Christensen 1989).

Auletta indicated that many in the underclass have become behavioral as well as income problems. Many prefer the ghetto streets and the quick rewards of crime. In his view, the poor are victims of their "poor" values, their uncaring or desperate parents, as well as of environmental neglect. The members of the underclass, mainly products of peer-oriented socialization, unrelated to the world outside of the ghetto and the welfare system, live diffuse and directionless lives, based on instant gratification, and unconcerned with the consequences of such activity in the near (let alone distant) future.

Most of the members of the underclass, and of others in the middle class, who are in-training for downgrading, all suffer from a condition of existential nausea. In a world where one's basic needs of the moment are provided by welfare or the street, one has little incentive to prepare oneself or one's children for the unknown future. Some of the children of the rich also suffer from inappropriate family socialization, and thus the population is increasingly composed of individuals who have not internalized the values and skills of living in a productive peaceful self-sufficient society. As Sean O'Casey once put it, "all the world's a stage and all of us are actors, but too many of us are too bloody under-rehearsed (to live in a civilized society)."

The prospects for growth of the underclass, the ghetto, and dependent problem populations are growing. It can close off the ghetto, externally police it and subvert it as it currently does with the dependent Indian reservations. Murray calls this custodial democracy.

It can deal with the ghetto as physicians deal with the victims of a disaster—by selective triage and individualized rehabilitation services with those who can be adequately motivated for change.

Or, it can move to close off the growth of the inadequately socialized, along with selected policies to reverse the underclass generation process.

It is obvious that the underclass population, as a social problem, did not arise solely from a dysfunctionality of the social system. Neither was it solely a product of the disastrous effect of a welfare system which makes no requirements on the beneficiaries of welfare for change in their life patterns in order to prevent further dependency. There is much more involved in the causation of the problem. There was also the contemporary changes in family norms arising out of pressures from the women's liberation movements and the expansion of civil liberties in the United States. These resulted in a weakening in volume, depth and quality of the familial process of child socialization so necessary for preparation of children for participation in the civil and employment marketplace. Contemporary changes in the schools, which were faced with teaching inadequately socialized children, and based on inadequate theories of the educational process, has led to less effective training of workers and citizens, especially in the ghetto schools. Changes in institutional policy in local authorities which deal with families and youth, have legitimated formerly restrained behaviors leading to the proliferation of dependent female-headed families. Changes in the structure and policy of voluntary social agencies in the United States, the growth of the psychotherapeutic movement and the distancing of the social work movement from the poor have all contributed to the isolation of the underclass from the mainstream of society and its operational norms.

Centralization of welfare policies and the weakening of the discretionary powers and direction of local and state welfare agencies have all contributed to the growth of the underclass in the United States. The absence of a rehabilitative assignment for the welfare system, tying client grants to preparation for and acceptance of employment and effective socialization of children, has presented the recipients with a message encouraging the development of underclass lifestyles. The distancing, both geographical and social, of the successful components of ethnic and racial groups from their "brothers and sisters" in the ghetto have compounded the problem. And, above all, causative factors for the generation of an underclass lies in the conflict in a welfare policy which ignores economic problems.

In a competitive capitalist society, effective and usable products are sought out by buyers. Ineffective and unusable products have to be marked down as distressed merchandise.

New products, if they are to be sold, have to be improvements on the old, reflecting elimination of existent faults; and a competitive market requires more and more complex product preparation. Workers who have failed to effectively prepare themselves for adequately compensated employment are as unsalable in the market as shoddy products. Unlike products, however, people *can* be self-correcting, either immediately or intergenerationally, if they are motivated by external conditions to seek change in themselves. Similarly, if adequately prepared workers become unemployable, the next generation of prospective workers "gets the message" and prepares itself differently. But this does not occur if a welfare system and the society provide conditions which inhibit the process of such self- correcting change. Thus, the necessary buildup of human capital is avoided among the members of the underclass by interaction with the social system and its welfare agencies which inhibit the development of productivity among the underclass.

America needs to face the fact that there is a complex of destructive interactive factors which support the generation of a growing underclass. These factors have a damaging effect on a major sector of the population and disturb the operation of the functioning society. These disturbing factors include the underclass culture, the ghetto, violent crime, drug sale and use, broken families, ill health and many others. The promotion of sexual and parent liberation without responsibility has permeated the American culture to the point that in some intellectual circles responsible family life is viewed as deviant behavior. This complex of destructive factors needs to be seen for what it is. These factors serve to divide the nation into two sectors: the productive sector and the destructive sector. Only when a society agrees to the definition and causes of its problems can a solution be chosen and a consensus built to apply the solution.

In my opinion, when the solution is determined, it will involve the rebuilding of the traditional family, the neighborhood school and the local religious institution. Without these as a foundation, this civilization and productive society are doomed. Only when a consensus on the solution is finally arrived at can social policy reshape the rules of social functioning, with incentives and rewards for those who build family life and local social control, and powerful disincentives for those who do not.

# REFERENCES

Albrecht, J.W., "Negative Taxation and Divorce in SIME/DIME," *Journal of the Institute for Socio-Economic Studies*, 1979, vol. 4, no. 3, 75-82.

Auletta, Ken, *The Underclass*, New York: Random House. 1982.

Beck, Allen J. and Susan A. Kline, "Survey of Youth in Custody, 1987," U.S. Dept. of Justice, Bureau of Justice Statistics, Sept. 1988, 1-2.

Berger, Brigitte and Peter, *The War Over the Family: Capturing the Middle Ground*, Garden City, New York: Anchor Press/Doubleday. 1984.

Bernstein, Blanche, *The Politics of Welfare: The New York City Experience*, Boston: ABT Books. 1982.

Blum, Richard H., et al., *Horatio Alger's Children*, San Francisco: Josey-Bass. 1969, 47, 58, 69, 71, 89, 91-93.

Bode, J., *Kids Having Kids*, New York: Watts Publishing Company. 1980.

Brown, B. Frank, "A Study of the School Needs of Children from One Parent Families," *Phi Delta Kappa*, April 1980, 537-540.

Cantor, Rachelle J., "Family Correlates of Male and Female Delinquency," *Criminology*, (20). 1982, 149-167.

Carlson, Allan C., "Between Parents and Pushers: Resolving America's Drug Crisis," *The Family in America*, Rockford Institute, Rockford, Illinois, vol. 2, no. 7, July 1988.

Chapman, Bruce, "Fairness for Families: An Organizing Theme for the Administration's Social Policies," *The Journal of Family and Culture*. (2) 1986, 23.

Cherlin, A.J., *Marriage, Divorce and Remarriage*, Cambridge, Massachusetts: Harvard University Press. 1981.

Christensen, Bryee J., "From Home to Prison Life: The Roots of American Crime," *The Family in America*, Rockford Institute, Rockford, Illinois. April 1989, vol. 3, no. 4, 1-8.

Cornell, Dewey G., et al., "Characteristics of Adolescents Charged with Homicide: Review of 72 Cases," *Behavioral Sciences and the Law* (5) 1987, 11-23.

Danziger, Sandra, "Breaking the Chains: From Teen-Age Girls to Welfare Mothers, Or Can Social Policy Increase Options," chap. 5 in Meyer, Jack A., ed., *Ladders Out of Poverty*, Washington, D.C., American Horizons Foundation, 1986. (Also available from Institute for Research on Poverty, Discussion Paper #825-86.)

Danziger, Sheldon, "Overview" in Special Issue. Defining and Measuring the Underclass, *Focus*, vol. 12, no. 1. Spring and summer 1989, Madison, Wisconsin, Institute for Research on Poverty, University of Wisconsin.

Dornbusch, Sanford M., et al., "A Report to the National Advisory Board of the Study of Stanford and the Schools on the Main Findings of our Collaborative Study of Family and the Schools," Stanford, California, Stanford University Department of Sociology, Feb. 27, 1986.

Forman, Rachel, Z., *Let Us Now Praise Obscure Women: A Comparative Study of Publicly Supported Mothers in Government Housing in the U.S. and Britain*, Washington, D.C.: University Press of America. 1982.

Glueck, Sheldon and Eleanor, *Family Environment and Delinquency*, Boston: Houghton Mifflin. 1962, 221.

_____, "Working Mothers and Delinquency," in *The Sociology of Crime and Delinquency*, Marvin E. Wolfgang, Leonard Savitz and Norman Johnston (eds.), New York: John Wiley and sons. 1970, 497-498.

_____, *Unraveling Juvenile Delinquency*, Cambridge: Harvard University Press. 1950, 88-91.

Gove, Walter R. and Crutchfield, Robert D., "The Family and Juvenile Delinquency," *The Sociological Quarterly* (23) 1982, 301-319.

Hirschi, T., "Crime and the Family," in James Q. Wilson (ed.), *Crime and Public Policy*, San Francisco: Institute for Contemporary Studies. 1983, 53-58.

Hirschi, Travis and Selvin, Hanan C., "False Criteria of Causality in Delinquency Research," *Social Problems* (13) Summer 1965, 254-256.

Ianni, Francis A., *The Search for Structure: A Report on American Youth Today*, New York: Free Press. 1989, 175-210.

Klausner, S.Z., *Six Years in the Life of the Impoverished: An Examination of the WIN Thesis*, Philadelphia: Center for Research of the Acts of Man. 1978.

Knight, Raymond A. and Prensky, Robert A., "The Development Antecedents and Adult Adaptationsx of Rapist Subtypes," *Criminal Justice and Behavior* (14) 1987, 403-426.

Lewis, Oscar, *La Vida*, London: Panther Press. 1968.

_____, *A Study of Slum Culture: Background of La Vida*, New York: Random House. 1968.

Marsiglio, William, "Adolescent Fathers in the U.S.: Their Initial Living Arrangements, Marital Experience and Educational Outcomes," *Family Planning Perspectives* (19) 1987, 240-251.

McLanahan, Sara S., "Family Structure and Dependency: Early Transitions to Female Household Headship," *Demography* (25) February 1988, 1-16.

Mead, Lawrence M., "The New Welfare Debate," *Commentary*, March 1988, vol. 85, no. 3.

Murray, Charles, *Losing Ground: American Social Policy, 1950-1980*, New York: Basic Books. 1984.

Nisbet, R.A., *Community and Power*, New York: Oxford University Press. 1953.

Pirog-Good, Maureen A., "Teen-age Paternity, Child Support and Crime," *Social Science Quarterly* (69) 1988, 527-547.

Popenoe, David, *Disturbing the Nest: Family Change and Decline in Modern Society*, New York: Aldine de Gruyter. 1988, 168-187, 196-197, 222, 237- 239.

Sampson, Robert J., "Does an Intact Family Reduce Burglary Risk for Its Neighbors?" *Sociology and Social Research* (71) April 1987, 204-207.

Sandberg, Neil C., *Stairwell 7: Family Life in the Welfare State*, Beverly Hills, CA: Sage Publications. 1978

Segalman, Ralph and Basu, Asoke, *Poverty in America: The Welfare Dilemma*, Westport, CT: Greenwood Press. 1980.

Sharff, Jagna Wojcieka, "Free Enterprise and the Ghetto Family," *Psychology Today*, vol. 15, no. 4, March 1981.

Sheehan, Susan, *A Welfare Mother*, New York: New American Library, Mentor Books. 1976.

Smith, Douglas A. and Jarjouraj, G. Roger, "Social Structure and Criminal Victimization," *Journal of Research in Crime and Delinquency* (25) Feb. 1988, 27-52.

Stewart, Cyrus S. and Laenglein-Senger, Mary M., "Female Delinquency, Family Problems and Parental Reactions," *Social Casework* (65) 1984, 428-431.

Weitzman, Lenore J., *The Divorce Revolution*, New York: Free Press. 1985.

Wrong, Denis, "The Great American Trouble" (Review of *Crime and Human Nature* by James Q. Wilson and Richard J. Hernstein and "Confronting Crime: An American Challenge" by Elliott Cursie, in *The New Republic*, Jan. 20, 1986, 27-32.

_____, "21 Years Later: *Family and Nation*, Review of book by Daniel P. Moynihan, *The New Republic*, March 17, 1986, 30-33.

# CHAPTER 6

# WELFARE IN EXCELSIS

*W. T. Roy*

> Bowed by the weight of centuries he leans
> Upon his hoe and gazes on the ground,
> The emptiness of ages in his face,
> And on his back the Burden of the World.
> Who made him dead to rapture and despair,
> A thing that grieves not and that never hopes,
> Stolid and stunned, a brother to the ox?
>
> —*The Man With The Hoe*, Edwin Markham (1852-1940)

The author of these evocative opening lines of a rather long poem went on to predict the mass uprising of plundered, profaned and disinherited masses everywhere, to overthrow their oppressive rulers and achieve social and economic justice long denied them. Unfortunately, he lived long enough to see his apocalyptic vision shattered by the rise and establishment of equally horrendous tyrannies, in the name of doctrinaire racist or communist ideologies, and extended to areas and populations that had known naught of either.

These totalitarian régimes seemed to negate the optimistic liberal political theories of the Enlightenment, which had confidently predicted the inexorable progress of mankind from the oppressions of the Ancien Regime and its counter-parts to sunlit uplands of democratic and admirably just utopias. This enhancement was to be the result of techno-logical advances (providing larger surpluses of consumer goods than had ever been possible before) combined with utilitarian assumptions of rational hedonistic behavior on the part of everyone, guaranteeing optimum distribution of the material benefits of technology. All of this was to be enshrined in laws guaranteeing a package of 'inalienable rights', and thus, once and for all replacing outmoded traditional (or even charismatic) régimes with rational-legal ones, based on impersonal, though utterly just, bureaucratic management of society. It seemed indeed that the Enlight-enment dream of a genuine *homo politicus* had been aborted by the irrationality or sheer bloody-minded egotism of a deviant few.

Even in those exceptional instances—the 'Western democ-racies' of the USA, Great Britain and some of its former Dominions—where the trappings of representative democracy had survived the political depredations of two world wars, the liberal dream was badly warped by the appearance of a strong modifying principle or force. This was none other than what the genius of Alexis de Tocqueville had identified nearly two centuries earlier in the nascent democracy of an infant United States of America. This he described in memorable terms as the 'tyranny of the majority' proceeding from the 'unreflect-ing passions of the multitude'. In short, these unreflecting passions are the very seedbed of irrational and frequently unfulfillable demands on decision-making authorities. Such pressures completely sabotage, or even pre-empt, any policies, based on rational economic analyses, aimed at providing just those conditions of economic and social justice, that members of democratic societies consider to be the core of their inalienable rights.

Of course there *is* an alternative scenario, the basis of which was first sketched by Aristotle, and followed up by a long succession of Western *savants* pronouncing on the conditions desirable in a society that seeks a liberal democratic polity that actually works. These conditions are really quite basic—a reasonably equitable, but by no means uniformly even, distribution of material and human resources; a literate and reasonably informed, but by no means specifically *politically* educated electoral mass; a class of professional politicians skilled and practiced in the act of decision-making, on the basis of accurate information and rational analysis, but by no means unwilling to compromise if necessary, without regarding it as personal defeat; a bureaucracy skilled in the implementation of executive decisions, though, at the same time, capable of influencing those decisions with inputs of well-considered counsel on the basis of long experience, but by no means succumbing to the temptation to use this influence to personal advantage; the existence of an opposition in the role of watchdog, but by no means that of gadfly; the existence among the electoral mass of a sense of personal efficacy in the political process (be it only well-considered voting), combined with sufficient trust in the integrity and capability of the decision-makers to leave them to do their job once installed in office; and last, but by no means least, a responsible media, which restrains itself (in conditions where externally imposed censorship is absent) from muckraking and demagoguery in carrying out its major function of providing information and analysis as distinct from titillating trivia about the private concerns of public personages.

Should this seem a daunting catalogue of desirable but in practice unattainable virtues, then one must come to the conclusion that a long series of observers and commentators (some of whose most recent members include such notables as Dahl, Finer, Schumpeter, Almond, Verba and Crick) are wild-eyed utopians out of touch with social and political reality in the societies to which they belong. Nevertheless, it must be admitted that the simultaneous presence of *all* these factors in any single society in Western liberal democracies is a rare occurrence indeed. In fact, in *some* the practices of *some* sectors and *some* individual participants in the political process have produced effects highly dysfunctional to achieving the eminently worthy end of equitable distribution of goods and services.

This arises from the infiltration of the educational system by a group of woolly-minded, gullible and occasionally venal preceptors, with libertarian as distinct from simply liberal ideas, propagating a doctrine of *inalienable rights alone* without any mention of *corresponding obligations* to the State that guards and guarantees those rights. This skewed imbalance of emphasis has, in some societies, produced a whole generation of enfranchised, but basically disenchanted and even cynical citizens, who nevertheless are conditioned and habitual dependents of the polity that is popularly called The Welfare State. The prospects for liberal democracy continuing to survive in this milieu must now be scrutinized, since clearly the presence in its midst of a cohort of parasites battening on its bounty must at the very least vitiate and at worst mortally threaten its very existence.

## WELFARE IN EXCELSIS—
## THE ACHILLES HEEL OF LIBERAL DEMOCRACY

'Welfare' is a need common to all societies, because of the existence in all societies of individuals incapable of surviving on their own efforts alone—the very young, the sick and aged, the physically and mentally handicapped, and also those who, through no fault of their own, are without access to means of subsistence, such as land or remunerated employment.

The commonest source of welfare was, and in many societies still is, the kinship group. This is institutionalized and built into the value systems of major Asian societies, for example, China and India, in the form of filial piety. In the medieval West, after the widespread adoption of Christianity, additional sources of welfare were the Churches and private charity. This was adequate for small populations, with no great surpluses to distribute, but periodically decimated by Malthusian checks—war, famine and pestilence—which brutally restored the balance between numbers and resources.

However, technological advances in the eighteenth and nineteenth centuries, in both agriculture and industry, resulted in the accumulation of means of production in a few hands, and the presence of ever-increasing surpluses of saleable goods. This was at the cost of a corresponding and increasing disparity in real incomes and patterns of consumption between the rich and the poor. The resulting fear entertained by the rich of the increasingly numerous poor was the prime reason for State intervention to defuse what was seen as a potentially revolutionary situation.

The instruments were a series of Poor Laws (in Britain) and similar enactments on the Continent during the eighteenth and nineteenth centuries. It was clearly understood by those enacting relief measures that this was not an act of meritorious charity or even of social justice, but simply of self-preservation. A prime example is the Bismarckian system of old-age and sickness benefits for the working class in Germany. This was designed to pre-empt the blandishments of Bismarck's *bête noir* the Social Democratic Party of the time.

The outstanding characteristic of this period of welfare was a clear determination that benefits should not exceed rigidly determined levels of mere subsistence. 'Frills' to enhance the quality of life were specifically excluded. Thus, the iron-hearted bigotry of the early Industrial Revolution— 'he who *does not* work, neither shall he eat' was modified to the more humane, 'he who *cannot* work, neither shall he starve'. And this is the way things remained in the Western world until World War II. It was then that the concept of welfare changed radically, and, led by Britain, most societies (including even a reluctant USA—that archetype of competitive individualism and self-reliance) adopted measures that went far beyond the mere relief of acute want. The doctrine of the State's responsibility to care for all essential needs of its citizens, from the cradle to the grave, was firmly established. What caused this change?

First, as a result of World War II, there have been tremendous advances in Western technologies that really *did* hold promise of great surpluses, which not only guaranteed profits for capitalist owners, but left plenty over to be distributed to the rest of the population.

Second, there was the emergence of secular humanism, supplanting the religious values of an earlier age, which had made private charity not only meritorious but very nearly obligatory. The core of humanist doctrine was the assumption that *every* human being was endowed with something called Natural Rights (now renamed Human Rights). This exalted the individual above the State. Hence, the State was no longer regarded as a living organism (to which every citizen owed loyalty and discharged well understood duties), but instead was merely a mechanism or instrument to make sure that the Natural Rights of every citizen were guaranteed, protected and implemented.

The conjunction of these two factors, that is, distributable surpluses and a belief in State intervention to ensure such distribution, laid the foundation of the Welfare State in the immediate post-war world of the 1950s. Indeed, the promise of welfare was seemingly fulfilled—from infancy to old age the citizen was assured of subsistence, housing, medical and educational facilities and so on—in short, nothing less than a decent lifestyle in contradistinction to mere survival at a subsistence level. Accompanying this was the phenomenon of full employment, partly as a consequence of reduced work forces in countries whose populations had suffered heavy casualties during the war, and partly because of the appearance of a variety of new industries and occupations in technologically developed societies.

Liberal protagonists of the Welfare State were thus able to claim that their views had been amply justified, and critics of the system, both Conservative and Marxist, were temporarily silenced. However, this halcyon state of things was not to last. During the mid-1960s and early 1970s, in most liberal democracies implementing wide-ranging welfare policies, productivity began to drop, real economic growth slowed down, and ever-increasing unemployment reappeared. In short, the gilt was well and truly off the Welfare State gingerbread—and worse was to follow. During the 1980s, all these phenomena intensified, until the whole concept of Welfare was once again called into question or even roundly denounced both by the Right and by the Marxist Left. The former, on the ground that abundant welfare benefits offer an open invitation to dishonest exploitation and abuse by the venal, who are ever present in all societies. The latter, on the ground that welfare is but a veneer, ineffectually concealing the unchanged nature of capitalism. What *really* went wrong?

In the first place, unrestricted greed for profits on the one hand and unrealistically high wages on the other progressively reduced the distributable surplus. Second, the governments of Western Welfare States lost sight of the plain fact that there is a direct link between the ability to deliver welfare benefits and the economic base that provides the means to do so. State intervention in the affairs of society has largely been confined to the sphere of *consumption* (of benefits), while similar intervention in *production* is fragmented or even seemingly random. This piecemeal application of Keynesian economic doctrines is the Achilles heel of Welfare systems as they presently exist.

In short, because of this asymmetry between two cardinal areas of intervention, the State has deprived itself of the ability to match benefits rationally with surplus production. It is on this equation alone that the success or failure of intervention depends. Lacking such rationality, the Welfare State inevitably slides ever deeper into deficit financing of welfare benefits and seemingly appears headed for economic self-destruction. The first evidence of this actually happening is growing disruption in society culminating in an actual decline in public order and safety. This arises from the presence of substantial numbers of the enforcedly idle, some of whom relieve their boredom by mischievous or even criminal but always destructive actions.

During the early 1980s, as production dropped, economic growth rates slid to zero or below, inflation rose by leaps and bounds, and unemployment figures skyrocketed. Western societies began to exhibit signs of deep fissions. The unemployed, already accustomed to receiving various benefits as a right, found their governments progressively unable to continue delivering these supports. They, therefore, blamed the system of production and exchange (loosely termed 'capitalist' but more correctly 'industrialist') and those they saw as its manipulators solely for their own advantage, namely employers. These, on the other hand, viewed labor—particularly organized labor in militant unions—as at best uncooperative and insensitive to the realities of the marketplace, and at worst as subversives, who wanted the objectives of welfare carried to the absurd length of 'He who *will not* work, neither shall he need to'.

Thus, a confrontational political style has developed to wrack Western societies with social disruption and a corresponding decline in law and order. In some societies contemporary equivalents of the 'sturdy beggars' of Tudor and Stuart times have reappeared, brazenly living off welfare handouts and intimidating less predatory members of society and their own governments. This generates a backlash, where more conservative and increasingly frightened elements in society are questioning the instrumental role of the State, and calling for a reform of society in which Duties are stressed instead of merely Rights. This, in effect, calls for a revival of the Organic State and, as a logical consequence, implies considerable modification of the Welfare State, or even its total abolition in favor of a competitive free-market economy and appropriately restructured political institutions.

Is the welfare phenomenon in Western society, therefore, now doomed? Or perhaps, was it doomed from the start to be no more than a 'flash in the pan' because reality was only *temporarily* obscured by a transient period of postwar prosperity, based on a combination of circumstances unlikely to last, let alone recur?

Lest this be regarded as a Jeremiad, let it be added promptly that there *is* light on the horizon for welfare governments prepared to recognize the root cause of their failure, namely ill-balanced intervention in the processes of production and distribution, without clearly understanding the link between the two. Fortunately, models already exist to indicate that a compromise solution is possible, but *only* if all parties in the confrontational situation can be reeducated to recognize the mutual benefits of rational cooperation. In a measure, Sweden and Austria are Western examples. So also are Singapore, Taiwan, South Korea and Japan, but in the context of traditional cultural milieus that the West is unlikely to be able to replicate. This is because despotisms (no matter how benevolent or well disguised) or even merely authoritarian régimes, are clearly antithetical to Western liberal democratic values and norms. In all the above cases, involvement of all actors in the productive process—financiers, managers and workers—in planning and decision-making has resulted in a considerable measure of industrial harmony. In consequence, uninterrupted production provides substantial distributable surpluses to support levels of welfare that are both realistic and sustainable.

In short, then, the solution to the current dilemmas of the Welfare State is a corporatist one, in which confrontational politics is replaced by meaningful dialogue. This, by implication, is contingent on the voluntary and willing surrender by *all* parties of the prevailing shibboleth of inalienable Rights, and the equally willing assumption of reciprocal Duties. Such willingness must stem, not simply from moral considerations, but recognition that *rational* pursuit of self-interest by each

*123*

party (involving voluntary restraints on human greed) is not only very sensible but a very practical guarantee of attaining optimum benefit without inviting destruction at each other's hands. Hopefully, this attitude of enlightened self-interest will enable economically realistic but still acceptable levels of welfare to be maintained. Nevertheless, for this a price will have to be paid, and that price is that society will have to recognize (however ruefully) and learn to live with the truth of Dostoyevski's somber dictum, which effectively demolishes the utopian form of liberal democracy that has flourished briefly as the Welfare State:

Bread and Freedom are together not compatible!

Notwithstanding this somewhat doleful prospect as a consequence of welfare *in excelsis*, we must remember that *no* situation (political or otherwise) is immutable. So, perhaps we ought to take heart from an observation made by that wise and insightful observer of the Human Situation, W. Macneil Dixon, who, in his Gifford lectures delivered under that title in 1935-1937, said:

Men are by nature striving, heroically stubborn as is
the mind itself
    Still nursing the unconquerable hope,
    Still clutching the inviolable shape.
They love best what they do for themselves, for what
they themselves make they have a great affection; what
is given out of charity they value less.

Let us hope Dixon was right, and on this hope let us rest.

# CHAPTER 7

# ETHNIC MINORITIES AND WORK

*Walter E. Williams*

In most public policy debates, discrimination is seen as the dominant reason for the differential performance of minorities in the labor market. Nobody will deny there is discrimination, neither would we deny that discrimination has effects on the outcomes observed. The important question, from a policy perspective, is how much of what is seen can be explained by racial discrimination and how much can be explained by factors other than race? This important question must be addressed. If discrimination explains relatively little of what we see, then resources expended to fight discrimination might be more productively deployed elsewhere.

One should always question differences in income, occupational status and employment "explained" by allegations of racial or sex discrimination. In the United States, for example, it is claimed that equally productive minorities and women earn only 59 percent of the income of white males. This allegation, taken at face value, means that in the name of protecting the "brotherhood" of white male workers, employers are foregoing large profits by paying wages 69 percent higher than if they would only hire the equally productive minority or female.[1]

If businessmen were actually doing that, one is left with the question: How could such a practice persist in relatively open markets? That is, if equally productive minorities and women were available for wages 69 percent less than their white male counterparts, then there would be a huge profit potential to be exploited by a non-discriminator, including minorities and women. Non-discriminators could simply hire the equally productive minorities and women at a lower wage and drive their competition out of the market through lower product prices. Companies have wound up on the industrial trash heap simply because their costs were a mere two percent higher than their competition.

In all likelihood, discrimination alone cannot explain large income differentials. A more probable explanation has its roots in human capital differences, that is, skills and talents. In the U.S. there are large human capital differences between blacks and whites. High school dropout rates among blacks, in some cities, exceed 50 percent. Even when blacks do graduate from high school, often their reading, writing and computational skills are less than those of an eighth grader. The latter observation suggests nothing less than gross educational fraud where schools certify, through awarding a diploma, a youngster as having attained twelfth grade skills, when in fact he has just a little more than elementary school skills.

Low skills and academic fraud stand out in stark relief when we examine the results of the college admission Scholastic Achievement Test (SAT) scores. In 1983, nationally, only 66 out of 71,137 (less than a tenth of 1 percent) black college-bound seniors scored 699 or higher out of a possible 800 points on the verbal portion of the test, and fewer than 1,000 scored higher than 600. On the mathematics portion of the SAT, 205 blacks had scores 699 or over (0.003 percent), and fewer than 1,700 achieved 600 or higher.

By contrast, 496 of the 35,200 (0.014 percent) Asians taking the test scored 699 or higher on the verbal portion and

3,015 scored 699 (0.09 percent) on the mathematics portion. Of the 963,000 whites taking the tests, 9,028 scored 699 or higher on the verbal portion (0.009 percent) and 31,704 scored over 699 on the mathematics portion (0.03 percent).

Poor black performance on standardized tests is frequently dismissed as "cultural bias" of the test. This charge raises Several questions. First, it is impossible to devise a culture free test. Second, Asians who are far more culturally distinct than any other group in the U.S. do better on both sections of the test than other American minorities; on the mathematics section, they do better than Americans in general. Third, those who make the charge of cultural bias cannot identify the specific test questions that are biased.

The cultural bias charge is without merit but, more importantly, the charge diverts attention away from the real causes of black under-achievement, namely, poor education, low teacher expectations, and poor educational incentives established by families. Instead of poor test performance focusing attention on these problems, the presumption of discriminatory tests leads to resources spent requiring colleges to have special admittance policies and racial quotas. These policies only superficially deal with the problems of black college attendance. When black students flunk out, in large numbers, colleges are often accused of insensitivity, lack of commitment or discrimination.

The educational deficiencies of blacks are not solved by four years of college. This is seen by even poorer performance by blacks relative to others on standardized tests such as the Graduate Record Examination (GRE), Medical College Admittance Test (MCAT) or Law School Admissions Test (LSAT), taken at the end of college for admittance to professional schools.[2]

## MINIMUM WAGE LAWS

In many instances, blacks face a double-blind. First, they receive poor education in government schools. Then that poor education is aggravated by regulatory laws which reinforce the deficiency.

The minimum wage is one such law. For the most part, the stated intentions underlying support for minimum wage laws are quite noble, such as: preventing worker exploitation and providing for living wages and higher standards of living.[3] However, when we evaluate policy, questions of its effects are far more important than those of intentions.

The *effects* of legislated wage minima are seen if we put ourselves in the place of an employer and ask: If $4 an hour must be paid, no matter who is hired, does it pay to hire a worker so unfortunate as to possess skills that enable that worker to produce only $2 worth of value an hour? Employers, held to the market discipline of profits, will find that hiring such an individual is an unattractive economic proposition. They will not hire that individual. Therefore, legislated wage minima discriminate against the employment of low- skilled workers.

Individuals who are most likely to have low skills, relative to the rest of the labor force, are teenagers. Teenagers are low-skilled because they lack the experience, discipline and maturity of adult workers. Moreover, minority teenagers are even more representative of low-skilled workers because they not only share characteristics of teenagers in general, but they bear the additional burden of fraudulent education.

The statistical evidence tends to confirm the theoretical prediction about the unemployment effects of minimum wages. In 1988, general unemployment was 5.5 percent. The unemployment rate for white youths 16- 17 and 18-19 years of age was about 16 and 12 percent, respectively. Black teenage unemployment, in the same age groups, stood at 34 and 31 percent respectively.

Unemployment figures were quite different during earlier periods of our minimum wage history as shown in Table 1. In 1948, overall unemployment was 3.8 percent; that of 16-17 year-olds was a little more than two and a half times higher.

Noteworthy is the fact that black teenage (16-17) unemployment, at 9.4 percent, was *lower* than white teens (16-17), which was 10.2 percent. In fact, up to 1954, unemployment among black 16-17 year-olds was comparable to or lower than that of whites. For 18-19 year-olds, unemployment among blacks was only slightly higher than whites throughout the period. Massive unemployment differences between black and white youngsters did not settle in until the 1960s, 1970s, and 1980s.

Faced with this reversal in the unemployment picture for black youths relative to white youths, several questions arise. Can it be explained by racial discrimination? While not denying that racial discrimination plays a role in employment decisions, it would be difficult for anyone to make the case that employers are more racially discriminatory today than they were during earlier periods.

Can educational deficiencies of blacks explain the worsening employment picture? Here we encounter the same difficulty. It is not likely that we can explain lower black teenage unemployment by arguing that during earlier periods blacks had more and better quality education than their white counterparts.

The rise in unemployment came with significant increases in the minimum wage law and more extensive coverage of occupations by the law.

So far as racial differences in unemployment are concerned, one might legitimately ask: if discrimination does not explain much, why is it that the minimum wage law affects black youths more adversely than white youths? The observation is not inconsistent with what economic theory predicts about the effects of minimum wages. When wages are legislated, which exceed the productivity of some workers, firms will make adjustments in their use of labor. One adjustment is to not only hire fewer workers, but to seek, among those actually hired, the more highly qualified. For reasons already discussed, white youths more often than black youths have higher levels of educational attainment and skills.

## TABLE 1
### Comparison of Youth and General Unemployment by Race (Males)

| YEAR | GENERAL | WHITE 16-17 | BLACK 16-17 | B/W RATIO | WHITE 18-19 | BLACK 18-19 | B/W RATIO | WHITE 20-24 | BLACK 20-24 | B/W RATIO |
|---|---|---|---|---|---|---|---|---|---|---|
| 1948 | 3.8 | 10.2 | 9.4 | .92 | 9.4 | 10.5 | 1.11 | 6.4 | 11.7 | 1.83 |
| 1949 | 5.9 | 13.4 | 15.8 | 1.18 | 14.2 | 17.1 | 1.20 | 9.8 | 15.8 | 1.61 |
| *1950 | 5.3 | 13.4 | 12.1 | .90 | 11.7 | 17.7 | 1.51 | 7.7 | 12.6 | 1.64 |
| 1951 | 3.3 | 9.5 | 8.7 | .92 | 6.7 | 9.6 | 1.43 | 3.6 | 6.7 | 1.86 |
| 1952 | 3.0 | 10.9 | 8.0 | .73 | 7.0 | 10.0 | 1.43 | 4.3 | 7.9 | 1.84 |
| 1953 | 2.9 | 8.9 | 8.3 | .93 | 7.1 | 8.1 | 1.14 | 4.5 | 8.1 | 1.80 |
| 1954 | 5.5 | 14.0 | 13.4 | .96 | 13.0 | 14.7 | 1.13 | 9.8 | 16.9 | 1.72 |
| *1955 | 4.4 | 12.2 | 14.8 | 1.21 | 10.4 | 12.9 | 1.24 | 7.0 | 12.4 | 1.77 |
| 1956 | 4.1 | 11.2 | 15.7 | 1.40 | 9.7 | 14.9 | 1.54 | 6.1 | 12.0 | 1.97 |
| 1957 | 4.3 | 11.9 | 16.3 | 1.37 | 11.2 | 20.0 | 1.70 | 7.1 | 12.7 | 1.79 |
| 1958 | 6.8 | 14.9 | 27.1 | 1.81 | 16.5 | 26.7 | 1.62 | 11.7 | 19.5 | 1.66 |
| 1959 | 5.5 | 15.0 | 22.3 | 1.48 | 13.0 | 27.2 | 2.09 | 7.5 | 16.3 | 2.17 |
| 1960 | 5.5 | 14.6 | 22.7 | 1.55 | 13.5 | 25.1 | 1.86 | 8.3 | 13.1 | 1.58 |
| *1961 | 6.7 | 16.5 | 31.0 | 1.89 | 15.1 | 23.9 | 1.58 | 10.0 | 15.3 | 1.53 |
| 1962 | 5.5 | 15.1 | 21.9 | 1.45 | 12.7 | 21.8 | 1.72 | 8.0 | 14.6 | 1.83 |
| *1963 | 5.7 | 17.8 | 27.0 | 1.52 | 14.2 | 27.4 | 1.83 | 7.8 | 15.5 | 1.99 |
| 1964 | 5.2 | 16.1 | 25.9 | 1.61 | 13.4 | 23.1 | 1.72 | 7.4 | 12.6 | 1.70 |
| 1965 | 4.5 | 14.7 | 27.1 | 1.84 | 11.4 | 20.2 | 1.77 | 5.9 | 9.3 | 1.58 |
| 1966 | 3.8 | 12.5 | 22.5 | 1.80 | 8.9 | 20.5 | 2.30 | 4.1 | 7.9 | 1.93 |
| *1967 | 3.8 | 12.7 | 28.9 | 2.26 | 9.0 | 20.1 | 2.23 | 4.2 | 8.0 | 1.90 |
| *1968 | 3.6 | 12.3 | 26.6 | 2.16 | 8.2 | 19.0 | 2.31 | 4.6 | 8.3 | 1.80 |
| 1969 | 3.5 | 12.5 | 24.7 | 1.98 | 7.9 | 19.0 | 2.40 | 4.6 | 8.4 | 1.83 |
| 1970 | 4.9 | 15.7 | 27.8 | 1.77 | 12.0 | 23.1 | 1.93 | 7.8 | 12.6 | 1.62 |

| Year | | | | | | | | | | |
|------|------|------|------|------|------|------|------|------|------|------|
| 1971 | 5.9 | 17.1 | 33.4 | 1.95 | 13.5 | 26.0 | 1.93 | 9.4 | 16.2 | 1.72 |
| 1972 | 5.6 | 16.4 | 35.1 | 2.14 | 12.4 | 26.2 | 2.11 | 8.5 | 14.7 | 1.73 |
| 1973 | 4.9 | 15.1 | 34.4 | 2.28 | 10.0 | 22.1 | 2.21 | 6.5 | 12.6 | 1.94 |
| *1974 | 5.6 | 16.2 | 39.0 | 2.41 | 11.5 | 26.6 | 2.31 | 7.8 | 15.4 | 1.97 |
| *1975 | 8.1 | 19.7 | 45.2 | 2.29 | 14.0 | 30.1 | 2.15 | 11.3 | 23.5 | 2.08 |
| *1976 | 7.0 | 19.7 | 40.6 | 2.06 | 15.5 | 35.5 | 2.29 | 10.9 | 22.4 | 2.05 |
| 1977 | 6.8 | 17.6 | 38.7 | 2.20 | 13.0 | 36.1 | 2.78 | 9.3 | 21.7 | 2.33 |
| *1978 | 6.6 | 19.4 | 40.4 | 2.08 | 13.0 | 32.2 | 2.47 | 10.0 | 22.5 | 2.25 |
| *1979 | 5.8 | 16.1 | 34.4 | 2.14 | 12.3 | 29.6 | 2.41 | 7.4 | 17.0 | 2.30 |
| *1980 | 7.1 | 18.5 | 39.7 | 2.15 | 14.5 | 36.2 | 2.5 | 11.1 | 22.3 | 2.01 |
| 1981 | 7.6 | 19.9 | 43.2 | 2.17 | 16.4 | 39.2 | 2.39 | 11.6 | 26.4 | 2.28 |
| 1982 | 9.7 | 24.2 | 52.7 | 2.18 | 20.0 | 47.1 | 2.35 | 14.3 | 31.5 | 2.20 |
| 1983 | 9.6 | 22.6 | 52.2 | 2.3 | 18.7 | 47.3 | 2.53 | 13.8 | 31.4 | 2.28 |
| 1984 | 7.5 | 19.7 | 44.0 | 2.2 | 15.0 | 42.2 | 2.8 | 9.8 | 26.6 | 2.71 |
| 1985 | 7.2 | 19.2 | 42.9 | 2.23 | 14.7 | 40.0 | 2.7 | 9.7 | 23.5 | 2.42 |
| 1986 | 7.0 | 18.4 | 41.4 | 2.25 | 14.7 | 38.2 | 2.6 | 9.2 | 23.5 | 2.55 |
| 1987 | 6.2 | 17.9 | 39.0 | 2.17 | 13.7 | 31.6 | 2.3 | 8.4 | 20.3 | 2.42 |
| *1988 | 5.5 | 16.1 | 34.4 | 2.14 | 12.4 | 31.7 | 2.56 | 7.4 | 19.4 | 2.62 |
| 1989 | 5.3 | 16.4 | 34.4 | 2.10 | 12.0 | 30.3 | 2.53 | 7.5 | 17.9 | 2.39 |
| 1990 | 5.5 | 15.9 | 38.9 | 2.44 | 13.1 | 28.2 | 2.15 | 7.6 | 20.2 | 2.66 |
| 1991 | 6.7 | 19.4 | 39.0 | 2.01 | 16.3 | 35.2 | 2.16 | 10.2 | 22.4 | 2.20 |

*Shows change in the federal minimum wage law.

Source: Bureau of Labor Statistics (Adapted).

*Handbook of Labor Statistics 1975* (Washington, D.C.: U.S. Government Printing Office), pp. 153-55.
Bureau of Labor Statistics, Bulletin 2307, August 1988 (Washington, D.C.: U.S. Government Printing Office).
Bureau of Labor Statistics, Bulletin 2340, August 1989 (Washington, D.C.: U.S. Government Printing Office), pp. 130-34
Bureau of Labor Statistics, Office of Employment and Unemployment Statistics, 1992

Therefore, a law that discriminates against the employment of low-skilled people can be expected to have a harsher effect on black youths compared to white youths.

Substitution of higher skilled workers for lower skilled workers is not the only employer response to legislated wage minima. Minimum wages cause employers to make other substitutions such as: automatic dishwashing machines for hand washing; the use of disposable cups, plates and utensils; the switch from salespersons to self-service; elimination of theater ushers, the switch from full service to self-service gasoline stations, and so forth. These are all possible and predictable responses to legislated wage minima whereby employers seek to economize on labor cost.[4] Moreover, employers can also respond by moving their manufacturing operations overseas to lower labor cost countries.

## ANTI-DISCRIMINATION LAWS

Legislated minima are not the only barrier to unemployment. There are numerous labor laws, written in the name of helping, which actually hinder the category of workers whom employers see as less preferred. To develop this argument, we will use a non-labor market example.

Consider the new supermarket that enters a neighborhood which has developed shopper loyalty to the incumbent supermarket. The new seller is faced with the challenge of piercing that loyalty. He must find ways to attract customers. Most often, the seller will offer something extra such as: special services, free items, special coupons, prizes and lower prices. Through this strategy, customers are encouraged to experiment with the new supermarket and become patrons.

Consider now the types of regulations that might frustrate the supermarket's efforts to become "employed" in the new neighborhood. One handicap would be legislation requiring the new entrant to charge the same prices as the established supermarket. Another would be to require the new supermarket to maintain the same hours of operation and provide the same services as the established market. Perhaps most damaging would be a law mandating that once a customer shopped at the new supermarket he could not change his mind if he deemed the services unsatisfactory or, somewhat less severe, requiring that customers go through a costly process, entailing legal fees and time, to prove the new supermarket unworthy, that is, "fire" the supermarket. While these seller handicaps would be deemed farfetched applied to a supermarket, they are not so farfetched in labor markets.

Let us examine seller handicaps in the labor market; after all, a worker is a seller who can be handicapped as well. Quite often, employers have preconceived, perhaps erroneous, notions about the productivity of minority workers. These notions may stem from lack of experience with minority workers and racial stereotypes. In many cases, the minority worker, like the supermarket example above, may be an "outsider" in the sense of not being acquainted with someone in the firm who would be able to vouch for his productivity, honesty, promptness and other desirable worker attributes.

If there are fixed entry level pay scales and work routines, as a result of law or collective bargaining agreements, the employer (buyer of labor) has reduced incentive to experiment with a worker who is perceived as risky in terms of productivity or has attended a school which has a reputation for mediocre students. This is true even if the minority worker is, in fact, just as good or better than the employer's general work force. The handicap is exacerbated if the minority worker has lower productivity.

The worker has no way to induce the employer to take a risk if entry wage levels are fixed. After all, why take the risk if other workers are available; what does the employer stand to gain? Thus, fixed entry wages tend to discriminate in favor of those workers who are perceived by employers as more preferred. This is identical to our example of the supermarket whereby a ban on lower prices and extra services would discriminate in favor of the already established supermarket because customers would have little incentive to experiment with the new (unknown) entrant.

There are labor laws and anti-discriminatory laws that make it costly for employers to dismiss workers whether the cause for dismissal is just or unjust. This means, when employers make hiring decisions, their calculation must also include the cost of firing. Because of anti-discrimination laws, a minority or female worker, who turns out to be a disappointing worker, may cost thousands of dollars to fire if the worker brings a charge of race or sex discrimination. Thus, an employer might be inclined to take a chance with a minority or female whose credentials or references are questionable, but because of high dismissal costs, he may opt not to take the risk and subsequently foregoes a chance to revise his *a priori* race-based perceptions about worker productivity.

Whether it is fair or not, for some workers to start out at a lower wage than others, or for employers to have greater freedom to dismiss a worker, is a question beyond the competence of economic theory. But economic theory can predict some of the consequences of not allowing some people to be free to charge a lower price for what they sell, and the consequences of not permitting employers the right to dismiss a worker without incurring large costs for doing so.

Just as in the case of minimum wages, the regulation of entry level wages tends to discriminate against the already handicapped and benefit preferred sellers who may very well recognize that benefit and make political efforts to impose the regulations.

## HIGH SKILLED VS. LOW SKILLED WORKERS

The following simple scenario is instructive. Consider that an employer can build 100 yards of fence by either of two techniques: Technique 1 requires the use of three low skilled workers who are paid $13 each. Technique 2 requires the use of one high skilled worker who is paid $35. Either technique provides the employer with the same 100 yards of fence.

Assuming the employer sought to maximize profits (minimize costs), he would use technique 2 because it would cost only $35 compared to $39 for hiring three low skilled workers at $13 each.

Now, let us assume that the high skilled worker demanded $55 a day. The employer would switch to technique 1, hiring the three low skilled workers, since by comparison it would only cost $39. It is a safe bet that the high skilled worker would anticipate this reaction. Therefore, before he demanded $55, he would organize other skilled workers to lobby for a minimum wage law, or entry level wages, in the fencing industry. The standard arguments would be "to provide for a living wage," "prevent exploitation," and if the low skilled workers were minority, "fight racism." With these arguments, the high skilled worker may generate enough political support for the enactment of a minimum wage in the fencing industry of say $25 a day.

After the minimum wage law is enacted, the cost to the employer of using technique 1 would be $75. Thus, the high skilled worker would stand a greater chance of successfully demanding $55 per day. The reason is that he has used the coercive powers of government to price his lower wage competition out of the market. It is worth noting that the minimum wage could have the same effect of pricing low skilled workers out of the market even if the intention was honestly meant to help low skilled workers.

Using government to price one's competition out of the market is a standard practice by sellers whether as sellers of labor, as in the case of unions, or sellers of finished products. Tariffs on foreign products, like automobiles, are an example. Domestic automobile manufacturers, along with auto unions, always lobby to have tariffs imposed on foreign autos. If they can use government to raise the price of foreign autos, they can charge more for domestic cars. That means higher profits for manufacturers and higher wages for union members. The only difference between lobbying for tariffs and lobbying for minimum wage laws is the rhetoric employed. That is, no American auto company or its labor union calls for higher prices for Japanese cars in the name of a concern for raising the living standards for Japanese auto manufacturers and their workers. They are more honest. They say it is to protect American workers and manufacturers from competition with foreigners. If the rhetoric behind union support for minimum wages was just as honest, supporters would reveal their protectionist desires.

## OCCUPATIONAL LEISURE

There are many businesses or trades that can afford opportunities for disadvantaged people. Businesses like taxicabs, beauty shops, or landscaping are ideal because they require only modest amounts of training and initial capital costs. Despite the fact that *real* entry costs are relatively low, there are significant, perhaps insurmountable, politically erected barriers to entry that often appear in the form of local regulations. A very good example of these barriers is the taxicab industry in the U.S.

It is estimated that the capital cost to become a taxicab owner-operator is about $5,000 which includes a down payment on a car, meter, radio and liability insurance. Most of this outlay is recoverable if the owner defaults, hence increasing the likelihood of bank finance. The business skill requirements are also minimal. Nothing more than the ability to operate a car and learn locations in the city is necessary.

The real barrier is that, in most cities, the taxicab industry is highly regulated. In some U.S. cities, there are numerical limits on the number of taxicab permits issued; others grant exclusive operating rights to one or more taxi fleet operators.

## NEW YORK CITY TAXICAB REGULATIONS

New York City represents one of the more egregious examples of taxi regulation. The Haas Act of 1937 set a numerical limit on the number of taxis that could legally operate in the city. No new licenses (medallions) have been issued, leaving the city with 11,787 taxis. The original power (in 1937) paid $20 for the license and a small annual renewal fee. The medallion itself, and the rights it confers on the owner, is private property and is transferable. As such, it commands a market price. In 1990, a New York taxi medallion commands the hefty price of $140,000.

The high price for a taxi medallion is easily explained. If the taxi industry was an open market, where all those who were willing and able to provide taxi services could freely enter, the value of a medallion would approach zero. However, since the government restricts entry, incumbent taxi owners have monopoly power and are able to charge monopoly taxi fares and earn monopoly incomes. Medallion prices represent and measure the present value of monopoly earnings. In other words, the medallion price reflects the value its buyer places on being able to operate in a government-protected monopoly market free from competitive forces that would exist if all potential taxi owners could enter.

## THE WASHINGTON, D.C. TAXI MARKET

The Washington taxi market differs from other U.S. cities; it is a relatively open market. In Washington, a taxi license costs $50 and the other entry requirements are minimal.

Washington's relatively open market produces several predictable effects. The first of these is the number of taxis per thousand of the population. In Washington, there are 12.1 taxis/1,000 compared to New York City where there are 1.5/1,000. In fact, Washington has the highest taxi/population ratio in the nation. Second, taxi fares in Washington, D.C. are among the cheapest in the nation. Third, and of considerable interest for our topic, is that there is extensive black taxi ownership. In Washington, D.C., about 75 percent of its taxis are owned by blacks.

This observation points to some of the problems of the standard civil rights approach. A typical civil rights advocate will observe that there are relatively few black taxi owners in cities like New York and Philadelphia. For him, that means there is racial discrimination and he will seek a civil rights remedy such as quotas or setasides. However, racial discrimination may have little to do with his observation; it may have more to do with the rules of the game, that is, economic regulations. Black domination of the taxi industry in Washington cannot be explained by saying that racial discrimination does not exist in Washington. A far better explanation is the low entry cost compared to New York City.

Entry barriers in the taxi industry are just the most flagrant examples of what exists in many other markets that would otherwise provide a means to upward mobility for many disadvantaged people. Among the many licensed occupations are: cosmetology, landscaping, plumbing and street vending. Most often, the stated justification for licensing is that of protecting the public health and safety. Most often this is a ruse enabling the incumbent practitioners to restrict entry and provide for monopoly incomes.[5]

The solutions are obvious. In the case of taxis, for example, entry should have three requirements that serve the clientele interests: 1) the vehicle should pass a safety inspection; 2) the driver should pass a vehicle driving test; and 3) the owner shall have adequate vehicle liability insurance. The satisfactory performance of these requirements are the only ones that serve the interests of the riding public, not whether the owner can afford to purchase a $140,000 license.

Ways to break monopolies that have met with a limited degree of success in the U.S. have been that of challenging the licensing practice as a violation of antitrust statutes. Another more recent way has been to change the practice as being racially discriminatory in one form or another.

## THE MARKET VS. GOVERNMENT DISCRIMINATION

Despite the rhetoric often employed, market allocation of resources, rather than government allocation serves the best interests of discriminated- against minorities. This observation is not the same as asserting that when there is market allocation, there is no discrimination. What is being asserted is that discrimination has a cost borne by the discriminator when there is market, versus that of government, allocation of resources.

In the case of the minimum wage, consider there are two equally productive workers who differ only by race. Consider also that the employer is racially discriminatory and a statutory minimum hourly wage, or a union-management collectively bargained wage of $5 an hour must be paid.

If the employer must pay $5 per hour, how does he make his choice? The fact that all workers must be paid $5 an hour means there are no economic criteria the employer can select, assuming the workers are identical in terms of productivity. Therefore, the choice *must* be based upon non-economic criteria such as race, sex, nationality, nepotism, personal contacts, and other personal attributes of the prospective employee.

In the absence of a statutory minimum, a less-preferred worker could offset his non-economic disadvantages by offering to work for a lower wage, make what economists call a "compensating difference," offer to work for $4 per hour and possibly become employed. Thus, if the employer chose to discriminate against this less-preferred work, in light of the lower wage offer, it would cost the employer $1 per hour to indulge his taste for discrimination. However, if there is a statutory minimum hourly wage, it costs nothing for the employer to indulge his discriminatory tastes; after all, he must pay $5 an hour, no matter whom he hires. In that case, he selects the person whose non-economic characteristics are the most pleasing. Thus, discrimination is costless and the existence of a statutory minimum effectively eliminates the less-preferred worker's most effective method of competing with the more-preferred.

Some may argue that it is not fair that some people must lower their price in order to sell their product or service, or to raise their offer price to buy something. Economic theory has no special competence in evaluating arguments regarding fairness, but it can predict the effects of not allowing some people to bid a lower price for what they sell or a higher price for what they buy.

Consider the following question: Suppose one were to see a fat, old, ugly, cigar-smoking man married to a beautiful young lady; what assumption would one make about the man's income? Most would think his income to be pretty high, at least high enough to offer the beautiful young lady a "compensating difference." That is, the man may have purchased a grand house, a luxury car, jewelry and other inducements for the beautiful young lady.

Some people, having a misguided fixation with fairness, may conclude that it is unfair for beautiful young ladies to discriminate against fat, old, cigar-smoking men by charging higher prices. They may demand that a law be written to bring a halt to such practices. Once the law is enacted, what happens to the probability of a fat, old, ugly, cigar-smoking man marrying a beautiful young lady?

The law limiting his ability to offer a higher price eliminates his most effective method of competing with more-preferred men. In fact, the law would benefit more-preferred men to the extent it would eliminate some of their competition. The minima wage law has a similar handicapping effect, except that it is on the selling side of the market. Its handicapping effects are well known to racists in America and South Africa who have supported legislated minima.[6]

Government can play a role in the allocation of resources, which work to the disadvantage of the less-preferred, not only by mandating prices but through regulation of economic activity. Consider the following example.

A printing firm is faced with the choice of hiring two equally productive printers. The white printer demands $100 per day while a black printer is willing to work for $75. The firm's revenues, costs and profits are shown in Table 2.

| TABLE 2 | |
|---|---|
| Total Revenue | Total Costs |
| $300 sales | $ 75 wages |
| | $225 profits |
| $300 | $300 |

Assuming that the entrepreneur sought to maximize profits, he would hire the lower priced black worker and earn $255 in profits. To indulge his taste for discrimination would cost him $25 per day in reduced profits by hiring the higher priced white worker.

As shown in Table 3, we assume that the government imposes a 50 percent profit tax on the firm; all else remains the same. The imposition of the profit tax reduces the entrepreneur's property rights to profits, that is, the government owes part of whatever profits he earns.

| TABLE 3 | |
|---|---|
| Total Revenue | Total Costs |
| $300 sales | $ 75 wages |
| | $112.50 profit tax |
| | $112.50 profits |
| $300 | $300 |

Whenever there are changes in tax, we predict that people will seek ways to reduce their exposure to the tax, and therefore, keep a greater portion of the earnings. This response is shown in Table 4.

| TABLE 4 | |
|---|---|
| Total Revenue | Total Costs |
| $300 sales | $100 wages |
| | $100 profit tax |
| | $100 profit |
| $300 | $300 |

After the imposition of a profit tax, the entrepreneur will seek to capture part of his earnings in a nontaxable form. He may hire the racially more attractive employee. Before the profit tax, such an indulgence would have cost him $25 in foregone profit, namely the wage difference between the black and white worker. As shown in Table 4, after the profit tax, the entrepreneur foregoer only $12.50 in profits to indulge his discriminatory taste. That is, as shown in Table 3, hiring the equally productive black worker meant profits of $112.50; by discriminating against the black worker, shown in Table 4, the loss in profit is just $12.50, whereas before the imposition of a profit tax, the entrepreneur would have lost $25. Basic economic theory predicts that the lower the price of discrimination, the more people will take of it and the higher its price, the less people will take of it. Profit taxes lower the cost to discriminate.

Anything that weakens private property rights also weakens incentives to choose the most efficient ways. Since there are no private property rights and no money profits to decision-makers in government operations, one expects that government operations would take the lead in discrimination. There is little cost borne by the discriminator in government activities, which is not to say there is no cost, but it is borne by the general taxpayers. We might add that the government will be in the forefront of discrimination whether the political climate dictates discriminating *against* blacks and other minorities or dictates discriminating in *favor* of blacks and other minorities.

## CONCLUSION

Racial discrimination is offensive to civilized standards of conduct, fair play and justice. Despite our moral revulsion against its practice and those who engage in it, racial discrimination should always be seen as having an economic dimension as well. It costs something.

There are government actions advocated by people of evil will, often unwittingly supported by those of good will, that reinforce racial discrimination by making it less costly to its practitioners and, therefore, more costly to its victims. In general, it is those government actions that impede voluntary exchange and weaken private property rights that subsidize discrimination by lifting the cost burden of discrimination and spreads it to the victim and society at large.

To the extent that this proposition has merit, public policy should have a greater focus on the rules of the game (economic laws) than on the more traditional focus of enacting antidiscrimination laws. In fact, voluntary exchange and private property rights, along with the forces of the marketplace, are far more effective in policing discrimination—by placing its costs on the discriminator—than a political body could ever be.

## NOTES

1. That is ($1.00-.59)./59 = .69.
2. See Walter E. Williams, "Race, Scholarship, and Affirmative Action: Campus Racism," *National Review.* May 1989, 36-38.

3. In South Africa, however, racist labor unions have always supported payment of minimum wages (rate for the job) for blacks. Their stated motivation was to protect white workers from being underbidded by black workers who were willing to work for lower wages. See Walter E. Williams, *South Africa's War Against Capitalism*. New York: Praeger Publishing Company, 1989, esp., chapter IV.

4. Actually, it is incomplete to say that employers seek to economize on labor cost. Operationally, the "employer" is actually an employee of the customer who is ultimately the employer. Customers prefer low prices to high prices. In the face of higher labor costs, customers will patronize that "employer" who tries to implement cheaper productive methods simply because the final selling price is lower than otherwise would be the case. "Employers" who do not make the adjustment are effectively fired by the customers who no longer take their business to him. Similarly, "employers" who do not make the adjustment are fired as stockholders, who see return on equity diminish, who sell their holdings in the company.

5. See Simon Rottenberg, "Economics of Occupational Licensing," in *Aspects of Labor Economics*, A Report of the National Bureau of Economic Research. Princeton, New Jersey: Princeton University Press, 1962, 3-20.

6. A particularly instructive example is the Davis-Bacon Act which mandates "prevailing wages," which are in effect superminimum wages, on all federally financed or assisted construction projects. During the legislative debate, there were many allusions to racial bigotry. U.S. Congressman Allgood was quite specific, "That contractor has cheap colored labor that transports, and he puts them in cabins, and it is labor of that sort that is in competition with white labor throughout the country." *U.S. Congress, House, Congressional Record*, 71st Congress, 3rd sess., 1931, 6513.

# CHAPTER 8

# ADOLESCENT VIEWS OF THE ECONOMY

*Adrian Furnham*

## INTRODUCTION

It is not until comparatively recently that there has been much research on young people's understanding of economics and trade or their behavior as consumers (Lea et al. 1987; McNeal 1987; Sevón and Weckstrom 1989; Furnham and Stacey 1990). There are a number of reasons why the topic of economic understanding and education is an important, if empirically, neglected topic. First, it may be that adult habits of spending, saving, investing, gambling and purchasing are established in childhood or adolescence (Furnham and Lewis 1986). Second, from a teaching perspective it is crucial to teach economic concepts to children and adolescents on the grounds that their knowledge is not extensive (Ingels and O'Brien 1985; Leiser 1983); their buying power is considerable (Davis and Taylor 1979; Furnham and Thomas 1984b) and there is accumulating evidence that training at a young age is both possible and effective. Third, economic understanding is inevitably related to political behavior. While the relationship between political and economic attitudes remains debatable (Furnham and

Heaven 1988), it is most probable the two are related. An economically literate adolescent is no doubt a politically sophisticated one.

There appears to be a relative paucity of research on adolescent economic beliefs and values. This is perhaps surprising, as there are many reasons for wanting to know what adolescents know and think about the working of the economy. Two "practical" reasons seem obvious: first, adolescents have considerable buying power—for instance in America, children spend over $4 billion annually; teenagers spent over $40 billion in 1980; while British 5-16 year-olds had an estimated £780 million to spend in the early 1980's on preferred goods and services—and it is of considerable interest to people in trade to know how, where and why that money is spent. Second, teachers of economics are clearly interested in when, how and why economic concepts are acquired so that they may teach these concepts more effectively at the appropriate age (Kourilsky 1977; O'Brien and Ingels 1985, 1987). There are also many interesting *theoretical* questions concerning adolescent understanding and beliefs about the economy such as: at what age various economic concepts are grasped and what socialization experiences determine the extent and structure of economic beliefs. McNeil (1987) in fact listed 20 theses that could guide studies on children as consumers. He also noted the number of agents in the socialization process whereby children learn to become consumers: parents, peers, teachers, and business. An understanding of economics no doubt relates to what sort of employment a young person seeks out and their behavior at work.

## THE ACQUISITION OF
## SPECIFIC ECONOMIC CONCEPTS

A number of studies have made attempts to trace the development of certain specific economic concepts in different countries such as Egypt (Waines), Finland (Sevón and Weckstrom, 1989) and Great Britain (Furnham and Cleare 1988). They can be classified into three categories: studies on the understanding of *money* (its origins, functions, etc.); research into concepts associated with *exchange* (buying and selling, profit, banking, etc.); children's ideas of the causes of, and morality associated with, the *distribution of economic resources*, including young people's economic values.

**Money**

To a large extent, the beginning of economic understanding occurs with a child's use of money (Pollis and Gray 1973; Witroy and Wentworth 1983). Sutton (1962) asked 85 children randomly chosen from the first to sixth grades (approximately 6 to 12 years-old) 12 questions such as: How do people get money?, What is a bank?, Why do people save? and so forth. The 1,020 answers were categorized into six responses: no replies (1 percent); *precategorical stage* where objects are named but with little understanding of economic meaning (63 percent); a category of moral value judgments—good/bad, right/wrong—irrespective of economic function (18 percent); two *isolated acts*/factors that are economically significant are juxtaposed—for example, people save just by saving—(12 percent); two *acts involving a reciprocity* which cannot be explained by other economic relationships—if you put your money in a bank, you get more back—(5 percent); and the subjective explanation gives rise to the *objective*—the single act derives its significance from its position in a system of relationships that is no longer conceived of in an isolated way (1 percent). The results showed that age, intelligence and socioeconomic background variables did not significantly discriminate between the child's stage of understanding, yet various external stimuli and experiences were important in understanding the development of economic concepts.

Berti and Bombi (1981) attempted to ascertain Italian 3-8 year-olds' conceptions of money and its value. The children were shown a variety of coins and notes which they were asked to identify. They were then asked what (from chocolate bar to motor car) they could buy with this money and they took part in a shopkeeper game-sequence to determine how much the children would pay for a purchase (as a customer) and give change (as a shopkeeper). From the work of Strauss (1952) and others, they hypothesized various stages: (i) no awareness of payment (children do not pay in the shopping game or recognize money); (ii) obligatory payment (children recognize that the customer must pay but do not discriminate between various kinds of money); (iii) not all types of money can buy everything (children realize that not all money is equivalent since they deny that the proffered money cannot purchase a particular object); (iv) sometimes money is insufficient (children recognize that some things cost more and others less and that certain types of money are not sufficient); and finally (v) the correct use of change (children realize the excessive value of some money with respect to price, and give change). They found "the progression through the first four stages is developed around pre-operational thinking and precisely during that chronological period in which such thinking is dominant." In contrast, the fifth stage implies the use of logical and arithmetic operations (Berti and Bombi 1981, 1182).

In an earlier study, Berti and Bombi (1979) concluded that the idea of payment for work emerges from a background of spontaneous (and erroneous) beliefs developed by children to explain the origin of money. In effect, the concept is only acquired if a child occasionally notices that his parents (and other adults) take part in extradomestic activities. Only when the understanding of work is substantially developed does it support the spontaneous beliefs about the origin of money. It was also established that the link between money and work is initially understood asymmetrically. Children affirm that parents work for earnings but do not understand that there is a need for money which can be obtained through working.

This indicated the existence of systems of ideas that are relatively independent, although they possess certain facts in common.

To a large extent the child's and adolescent's first contact with the economic world is through money—receiving pocket money, watching their parents shopping, buying and in some instances selling goods; giving money in church or on the street and, most importantly, in the exposure to the media. Studies in this area have shown that, at an early age, money is imbued with value and meaning but that the role of money in the economic system is imperfectly understood. Young people have to understand the role and nature of money in society before they can understand more abstract economic concepts like profit, loss, etcetera. They need to know such things as: the role of money in obligatory payments, the fact that different coins and notes are of different values, that change can be and needs to be given where necessary, that income is taxed, that money can be stored and so forth. Once these concepts are mastered, the development of abstract concepts can occur.

### Exchange

A central concept in any economic system is that of exchange: the exchange of money or goods and vice versa (buying and selling); the temporary loaning of money (banking); motives for exchange (profit); price setting, establishing wage levels and inflation; and perhaps most importantly the exchange of labor for wages.

Central to any economic activity are *buying* and *selling*, which are fundamental transactions that are by no means easy to grasp. Furth (1980) has noted how difficult it is for the child to understand the transaction of goods. For instance, he/she must understand the origin of money; the function of change, the ownership of goods. Children must also integrate the payment of wages, shop expenses and the shopowner's money into the system in order to understand the pricing of goods. For Furth, there appear to be four major stages concerned with the understanding of buying and selling: no understanding; understanding of payment of customers but not of the shopkeeper; understanding and relating of both customer and shopkeeper payment, but not of profit; and the understanding of all these things, with the idea of profit. Even then it is not certain if and when children understand how goods are priced, the relationship between profit, pricing, sales, etcetera. Jahoda (1979) conducted two buying/selling studies—one involving role-playing and the other semistructured interviews—in order to investigate 6-12 year-olds' conception of *profit*. In the role-playing study, children played the role of shopkeeper and the experimenter those of customers and suppliers (farmers). The critical part of the role-play involved the child's realization that the price that one *bought* goods for was different from that which one *sold* goods for to the customer. Where the purchasing price was consistently lower than the selling price, the child was credited with an understanding of profit; when the two prices were consistently identical, lack of such understanding was recorded; and a mixture of responses was regarded as transitional. It seemed that it was not until the age of about 11 that most children began to understand the concept of profit. The second more detailed interview study showed the child's development from no grasp of any transaction system to the development of two unconnected transaction systems and finally to one integrated system. Younger children (6-9 years-old) simply described events and made up nonsensical answers on being questioned about profit, whereas older children tried to make sense of economic relationships but failed to arrive at the correct solution.

Jahoda (1983) replicated this study with young African children in Zimbabwe in order to test the hypothesis that, because of their great exposure to salient trading and bartering experiences, African children acquire the concept of profit more rapidly than European children. The results confirmed the hypothesis that being active in trading makes for an earlier grasp of the concept of profit. Indeed, the Zimbabwean children were shown to be significantly in advance of British children within the same age range. This would imply that experiential factors (notably taking part in the actual exchange) have an important part to play in the development of the concept of profit.

Jahoda (1981) followed up the study on profit with a study on children's conceptions of *banking*—a complex and often remote economic concept for children and adolescents to grasp. First, 11, 13 and 15-year-olds were put through the shop transaction study in order to ascertain whether the subject understood the notion of profit. They were then asked a number of questions about the functions of a bank, such as: Suppose I put £100 into a bank, and after one year I take the money out again, would I get more, less or the same? and: Suppose I borrow £100 from a bank to pay back after one year, would I have to pay back more or less or the same? The responses of the children fell into six categories: 1) no knowledge of interest (get back the same amount); 2) interest on deposits only (get back more but pay the same); 3) interest on both, but more on deposit; 4) interest the same on deposits and loans; 5) interest higher on loans-not fully understood; and 6) interest on loans-fully understood. The developmental trends were striking and highly significant, yet only a quarter of the 14-year-olds fully understood the function of the bank, with no increase for the 16-year-olds.

This study was, in fact, replicated by Jahoda and Woerden-bagch (1982) in Holland. They found that, while primary pupils in both locations overwhelmingly saw the bank as simply a place that keeps money, twice as many of the older Dutch subjects realized that one borrowed money from a bank compared with the older Scottish subjects. However, the authors concluded that the socio-cognitive pattern of development for economic ideas is much the same for all modern industrial societies. Ng (1983) replicated and extended Jahoda's (1981) study with 96 children, 6 to 13 years old, from Hong Kong. Although he found much the same developmental trend, a full understanding of the bank emerged at 10 while the idea of profit emerged at 6 years old. Thus for both concepts the Chinese children were more precocious than the Scottish (and Dutch) sample.

As in previous studies, Ng examined the dynamics of conflict between schemes in the child. For instance, to induce cognitive conflict the interviewer deliberately asked the child to explain how the bank obtained money to pay its employees, electricity charges, etcetera, while having the same interest charges on money lent and borrowed. Although the impact of this conflict instruction was not significant, it seemed to be useful in examining economic development. Ng (1983) concluded that Hong Kong children's maturity represents a case of socioeconomic reality (partly at least) causing or shaping socioeconomic understanding.

More recently Furnham (1989a) looked at 11-16 year-olds understanding of four exchange related factors—price, wages, investments and strikes. The price setting of products was the only real departure from a clear developmental trend, showing the oldest group as having the lowest understanding; that is, 15-16 year-olds thought that the government or manufacturers decide shop prices rather than shopkeepers. While having superior or comparable understanding to both 11-12 and 13-14 year-olds in virtually all other areas, in this particular area they have an inferior understanding, confirming that economic understanding is not in global terms with all areas progressing equally, but is subdivided into part systems which, ideally, will eventually merge together and become integrated into one whole system.

In accordance with Berti (et al. 1982), recognition of profit was inconsistent. Of 11-12 year-olds, 7 percent understood profit in shops yet 69 percent mentioned profit as a motive for starting a factory today, and 20 percent mentioned profit as an explanation as to why factories had been started. The figure for understanding shop profit is consistent with Jahoda's (1979) finding that around 11 is the age where this understanding starts to occur. However, it is clear that different conceptions exist for the three groups, and while the 11-12 year-olds have not yet had to confront any inconsistencies, in 15-16 year-olds this process *has* started to occur. Few of the adolescent subjects of any age group saw profit as a determinant of shop prices, but increasingly with age, subjects saw profit as something shopkeepers take from money they receive. Thus while understanding the process of profit making, its predetermined nature in the mark up of prices was not appreciated by 15-16 year-olds.

Inflation was not well understood, as Leiser (1983) found, with subjects of all ages confusing the causal with the descriptive. Most children said inflation was the rise in prices (a description), yet inflation was the most common reason given for *why* prices go up (a causal inference). However, older children showed wider, more integrated conceptions by being able to accommodate profit and price rises as two separate processes whereas 11-12 year-olds confused them more often. Similarly, older children understood market competition as the limiting factor in shop prices much more than younger children. This inability to comprehend macroeconomic phenomena is due to younger children being unable to appreciate the aggregate effect of individuals' actions. Conceptions are tied to the actions of only one individual, and only when reasoning develops can aggregate effects and macroeconomic changes be appreciated. In the absence of this understanding, younger children tend to view social relations as the result of the constraint and coercion of authority figures (Damon 1977), and economic transactions will often be seen in terms of moral or legal imperatives (Burris, 1983). Thus 27 percent of 11-12 year-olds gave moralistic reasons why shopkeepers did not ask for more money, saying it would be 'unreasonable' to 'too expensive', against 7 percent of 13-14 year-olds and no 15-16 year-olds.

*153*

Virtually all subjects understood the process of wages as payment for work by age 13-14. However, younger subjects saw the relationship in much more immediate terms than older subjects. The 11-12 year-olds tended to see the manager or the till as the origin of wages, whereas 15-16 year-olds primarily saw company profits as the origin. This illustrates how conceptions organized in terms of part-systems (company profit and exchange of work for money) are linked together to form one system. As the process continues, conceptions become more interlinked and integrated (Furth 1980).

With increasing age, adolescents understood more of the determinants of income, through even at 15-16 years, only the minority of subjects mentioned both type and quality of work as determinants. Burris (1983) found that the numbers mentioning amount of work as an income determinant dropped from age 11, being replaced by different emphases on the type of job people did. Congruent with Burris's (1983) finding, the proportion mentioning type of work increased steadily up to ages 15-16, whereas two-thirds of subjects mentioned it as an income determinant.

Almost all subjects suggested investing "unneeded" money in banks or shares in order to gain more money, though slightly fewer 11-12 year-olds did so than older subjects. Once again, incomplete understanding of the concept was shown in the different age groups, however, over 80 percent of 13-14 year-olds mentioned investment as a necessary prerequisite for starting a factory today, and over half of these age groups realized there were other things needed too, such as good ideas for products. Subjects thus did understand investment in factories and some aspects of entrepreneurship in the present and future, but not in the past, a similar finding to that of understanding profit.

There was a trend for older children to understand industrial relations more fully than younger children, such as why people go on strike. Interestingly, 13-14 and 15-16 year-olds emphasized union leaders' roles in decisions to strike, whereas 11-12 year-olds emphasized workers' roles, with only a small minority of the older groups putting forward the idea of both of them having a role. A possible explanation for this is the high profile given to union leaders in the British media (prior to 1980); it is generally the union leaders, not workers, who convey strike decisions to the public. As they get older, children have more interest in social events and more access to adult media, and may thus acquire this slant toward union leaders. Cross-national comparisons would be useful here.

Thus even for 16-year-olds, able to leave school, the understanding of economics and industrial relations is poor in many areas. It may be seen as desirable to improve this state of affairs, since, while work experience may be important in some areas, it is still not known which economic misconceptions are correlated by maturation and life experience. Many studies have shown that children can be taught economic understanding at school, often to levels thought beyond their development capability, by means of role play (Kourilsky and Campbell 1984), class discussion (Kourilsky 1977) or just by presenting the correct relevant information (Berti et al. 1986). To what extent working mature adults have a more comprehensive or veridical knowledge of the economy is of course in question.

It may also not be valid to assume similar developmental trends across industrial societies. What is important to know is how the exposure to *which* economic *activities* (buying, selling, investing, borrowing, work) at *which age* relates to *which aspect* of economic understanding. It is probable that the direct line of causality from economic activity to understanding is bi-directional, such that a grasp of a concept gives adolescents the confidence to partake in the economic activity, which in turn improves their understanding.

## Distribution and Ownership

A crucially important economic and political concept is that of ownership, particularly whether it is personal or national. Berti, Bombi and Lis (1982) argued that children pass from an initial stage of complete ignorance about the productive function of means of ownership to recognizing that various means have to do with work and money and the production of goods. When a coherent and comprehensive view of the network of economic exchanges has been formed, the child understands that the sale of produced goods permits the owner to realize a profit and pay his employees.

Over 120 Italian children were interviewed in their study in order to determine whether the child recognized the existence of an owner for various objects (e.g., a factory, a bus, a farm), who they were and how they became the owner; the existence of agricultural and industrial products of these objects and whose they were; and what advantage the child thought the owner derived from each means of production. Five distinct levels were distinguished: The owner is the person found in *spatial/temporal contact* with the production means (passengers own buses); the owner is the person who *exercises an appropriate use* of or direct control over the producing means in question (drivers own the bus); the owner is the one who not only directly uses the producing means in question but also *controls its use* by others (the boss owns the bus); the owner is clearly differentiated from the employee in that they have the *function of giving orders*; and the owner is at the *top of the hierarchy* of command, and the boss at an intermediate position between the owner and worker.

Five different levels for the perceived ownership of products were also identified. These include a stage where the children believe producers are owned by anybody, followed by a stage where they are seen to be owned by those closest to them or using them. At the final level, children realize that products belong to the owner of the means of production and that the employees are compensated for their work by a salary. Children's ideas about different production means develop with different speeds but through the same sequences. Furthermore, the parents also had a development view of their children in that parents of the youngest children said that they had not been told or asked about jobs and ownership, while the opposite was true for older children. To what extent the sociopolitical and economic beliefs of parents influence the speed and quality of acquisition of knowledge about ownership and justice is unknown but clearly important.

The concept of ownership/possession (Furby 1978; 1979; 1980) and the concept of theft and justice (Brown and Lalljee 1981; Irving and Siegal 1983; Siegal 1981) are clearly linked. Furby (1980) has proposed two basic motivations in acquiring possessions—the enhancement of feelings of personal efficacy and control over the environment-though these are influenced by various social and cultural factors. Furby (1978) has argued that one may take a life-span approach to the meaning and functions of possessions which change throughout the life span. In children, for instance, possessions become valued because they are a source of constant stimulation and they may become a weapon for controlling interaction in others. In America, McGrew (1972) has demonstrated the links between possession and social power in very young school children, which have been related to the source of conflict and the affirmation and denial of friendship.

The concept of *control* seems the most salient defining characteristic of possession across all ages, though the acquisition process shifts from being passive in young children (10 and under) to being more active in those over 10 years. With a more active approach to acquisition, there is the development of more powerful affect attached to the objects possessed. It is at this stage (about 11 years or over) that enhancement of personal freedom becomes an important reason for owning possessions. A further factor in young and older adolescents is the implication of power and status which goes with the ownership of certain specific possessions. Thus from adolescence onward, possessions enhance feelings of personal security and may become substitutes for unfulfilled desires (Furby 1978).

The concept of (private) possession is inextricably linked with the concept of theft. There has been a sizeable amount of literature on children's understanding of and attitude toward theft and criminal justice (Brown and Lalljee 1981; Irving and Siegal 1983). Most of this literature has concentrated on the extent to which children and adolescents use mitigating circumstances to diminish partially the defendant's ability to act in a responsible law-abiding manner. Using 15-17 year-olds in an open-ended free response paradigm, Brown and Lalljee (1981) found, for most crimes (including theft, breaking and entering), that the subjects could and did provide a number of mitigating circumstances including brain damage, passion, economic need, revenge, provocation and coercion. Irving and Siegal (1983), on the other hand, looked at the mitigating circumstances in children's perceptions of criminal justice for three types of crime: assault, arson and treason. They found that as subjects got older (from 7 to 17 years) they tended to make fewer legal judgments mitigated by a variety of circumstances and more judgments in which these circumstances do not apply. Overall, younger subjects tended to be harsher in their judgment; their leniency and mitigating circumstances were highly dependent on the situation.

More recently Furnham and Jones (1987) looked at the relationship between views of possession and theft. Four groups of children ages 7-8; 9-10; 12-13 and 16-17 completed a questionnaire based on the work of Furby (1980a,b) and Irving and Siegal (1983). The results demonstrated that possession concepts become more differentiated with age, focusing more on the importance of positive acquisition, single ownership and social influence. Attitudes toward theft crimes become more harsh even in the face of mitigating circumstances. This increased harshness may be understood in terms of possessions becoming progressively more a part of the self-concept. Thus theft and consequent loss to self leads to empathy with the victim and feelings of retribution for the thief.

The concepts of poverty, wealth and the distribution of incomes could also be said to be related to ideas of ownership. Psychologists in general have, unlike their many social science colleagues, dedicated little time to poverty—its definition, causes, and consequences. (Furnham and Lewis 1986). Even less has been done with young people; hence Siegal (1981) set out to determine children's perceptions and evaluations of adult economic needs. Adolescents aged 13-16 were asked to distribute token money to dolls dressed as a doctor, shopkeeper, bus driver and waiter, with the question: How much money does each need to take care of his children? They were also asked whether their (unequal) distributions were fair and about the amount of effort required in the various professions. The results showed that the youngest children did not realize that unmet needs exist while older children were divided on the issue of equality—some believed that needs should be met regardless of the bread-winner's occupational efforts, while others believed that inequality is fair and that effort and ability should be regarded irrespective of need. No clear factors discriminated between those in favor of equity versus equality.

Winocur and Siegal (1982) predicted that older adolescents would be more likely to base judgments on equal pay for equal work, while younger children would be more likely to advocate that pay should correspond with family needs. Further, they hypothesized that though girls may be more likely to treat male and female workers equally, they would be more conservative in their achievement judgments than boys. Although they found support for the former hypothesis, they did not find it for the latter. Thus concern for family needs appears to decline with age and objective work outcomes take precedence over need in adolescents' allocation of economic rewards.

## WORK AND EMPLOYMENT

Leahy (1981) examined the development of class concepts (specifically comparisons between rich and poor people) in cognitive developmental terms. Over 700 young people in four age groups (mean 6, 10, 14, 17 years) were interviewed and asked to describe rich and poor people and distinguish between them. The responses were classified into categories of person description, including peripheral (possessions, appearances and behavior), central (traits and thoughts) and sociocentric (life chances and class consciousness) categories. Lower and working class subjects were more likely than upper middle class subjects to mention life chances and thoughts in describing the rich and the poor, while upper middle class subjects were more likely than subjects from the other classes to mention the traits of the poor. In the older subjects there was an increasing tendency to view classes of rich and poor people as not only differing in their external, observable qualities, but as being different kinds of people. As children get older, they place more emphasis on individual differences in effort, ability and other salient personality traits.

Furnham (1982) sought to compare two groups of adolescent school children's (15-year-olds) explanations for poverty. Public or fee-charging school boys (primarily middle class) tended to offer more individualistic explanations for poverty (e.g., lack of thrift and proper money management; no attempt at self-improvement) than comprehensive (primarily working class) school boys who in turn tended to rate social or structural factors (e.g., failure of industry to provide jobs) as more important. These results have been found with adult samples (Furnham 1982). Yet it should be pointed out that comprehensive school boys saw both individualistic and fatalistic explanations as relatively unimportant in explaining poverty. That is, the major differences between the groups lay in the importance that they attached to societal explanation.

The estimates of annual incomes of the poor showed interesting results. Public school boys gave higher estimates than comprehensive school boys. By-and-large the estimates were rather low, in that many people on social security or supplementary benefits earn more money than those estimates. It is known, for instance, that children underestimate both poverty and wealth because of their own experience of money (Danziger 1958). Presumably, adolescents also tend to underestimate, but not to the same extent. Interestingly, more comprehensive school boys estimated the amount in weekly wages than public school boys, who in turn preferred to make estimates in terms of annual amounts. This may reflect what they have learned from their parents, some of whom are probably paid monthly (middle class) and some weekly (working class). Ideas about relative poverty and wealth appear more developed in adolescence than in early childhood and they necessitate a more global perspective on the distribution of wealth in the society.

Finally, a few studies have attempted to understand how children perceive and understand political and economic *justice.* For instance, Miller and Horn (1955) were interested in children's perceptions of *debt.* Similarly, a few studies have considered adolescent's knowledge of, and attitudes toward trade unions (Patterson and Locksley, 1981) but strictly these studies are more related to socio-legal attitudes than an understanding of economic issues.

With reference to ideas of economic justice Siegal and Schwalb (1985) conducted a cross-cultural study of the perception of economic justice among Australian and Japanese adolescents. They were interested in whether concerns for worker ability, effort and productivity (outcome) compensated for family need in the distribution of economic rewards. There were numerous cultural differences and, as predicted, older Japanese adolescents, compared with their Australian counterparts, were most willing to allocate a significantly greater income increment to workers with high family needs or lower ability. Furnham (1987) replicated this study comparing the beliefs of 15-18 year-old British and South African young people. The study demonstrated a marginal overall nationality difference, with South Africans allocating more money to workers overall than British adolescents. This may be due either to a minor artifact (the fact that the base rate sum was less realistic for South Africa than Great Britain) but may equally be accounted for by the fact that white South Africans are used to higher salaries than their British counterparts. As predicted, each of the four worker variables—effort, ability, outcome and race—yielded significant effects. This partly replicates the finding of Siegal and Schwalb (1985), but whereas they used need of workers as the fourth worker characteristic (or equivalent dimension), this study looked at the race of the workers. Overall, the white adolescents allocated more money to white than to black workers. This may be either due to actual discrimination on the part of white middle class adolescents or to the fact that they are simply reflecting the reality of the economic world as they see it in their respective countries.

These results make more explicable the cultural differences in reward allocation. South African adolescents have been demonstrated to be more conservative in their sociopolitical attitudes and to hold stronger just world beliefs than comparative British adolescents (Furnham 1985). Both conservatism (with a small c) and just world beliefs are closely associated with the Protestant Work Ethic (strong achievement motivation through work) and, indeed, there is evidence that South African students do have high scores. Thus it seems that prevailing sociopolitical norms may influence the development of belief systems which in turn influence the perception of economic justice. Siegal and Schwalb argue that 'a particular issue meriting attention is whether youths regard the norms of "equal pay for equal work" or "greater pay for greater need" as social conventions of universal moral rules' (1985: 324). These studies have suggested that neither apply universally and that whereas some societies are more predisposed to principles of equality of work rewards, others stress individual equity.

Studies on economic distribution and ownership have demonstrated that it is not until early adolescence that children begin to grasp the complexities and interrelatedness of the economic system. They tend to be very simple-minded in their conception of ownership and possession and make punitive judgments for theft which become more tolerant over time. There are clear developmental trends but experiential and educational factors affect children's habits, judgments, understanding and behavior.

## ECONOMIC VALUES

Recently O'Brien and Ingels (1987) set about developing a valid and reliable instrument to measure young people's attitudes and values with respect to economic issues—the Economic Values Inventory (EVI). This multi-dimensional (eight factor) instrument was shown to be, in part, related to the adolescents' formal education in economics, whether they had a full-time job, their socio-economic status, their political party identification, their sex, age and race. Their main hypothesis—that formal education in economics would influence student economics attitudes, was confirmed. Most of the research has been concerned with the development of this scale rather than testing any specific hypothesis, however it appears to be a robust and reliable instrument suitable for use in any developed capitalist economy.

In their original study O'Brien and Ingels (1985) divided the 42 items into eight subscales which were consistent and which had respectable internal reliabilities. The scales are described thus:

A. *Free Enterprise System* (12 items): the respondent asserts the need for hard choices in an economy of limited resources, the importance of saving, the valuable contribution of business to society, the importance of competition for keeping prices low, the importance of freedom of occupational choice.

B. *Trust in Business* (5 items): the respondent asserts almost unquestioning trust or faith in businesses as benevolent institutions that provide cheap, trustworthy, reliable goods and services.

C. *Economic Alienation and Powerlessness* (7 items): the respondent asserts that they feel alienated from their economy and personally powerless in the face of the economic system.

D. *Government Role in Social Welfare* (6 items): in this factor the respondent asserts that the government is responsible for the well-being of the least-well-off in society.

E. *Government Role in Price Setting* (2 items): in this short two-item factor the respondent is against any government involvement in setting prices.

F. *Unions* (3 items): the respondent expresses negative attitudes to powerful unions.

G. *Treatment of Workers* (4 items): the respondent expresses the view that most employees and workers in the country receive fair treatment.

H. *Economic Status Quo* (5 items): the respondent holds the opinion that resources and opportunities are unfairly distributed in the present economic system, and that the status quo should be changed.

Furnham (1987) examined the economic values of about 100 British young people (16-17 years old) and compared them with the findings of O'Brien and Ingels (1987) from America.

There was a mean difference of 1.5 or above on items: 6 (the Americans believed more than the British that it is the duty of people to do their jobs the best they can), 21 (the Americans believed more than the British that a person who cannot find a job has only himself to blame), 26 (the Americans believed more than the British that their economy needed more people who were willing to save for the future), 31 (the Americans believed more than the British that advertising helped consumers make intelligent choices), 34 (the Americans believed more than the British that the situation of the average person is getting worse, not better), 35 (the Americans believed more than the British that we'd all be better off if labor unions were stronger) and 36 (the Americans believed more than the British that if you have a valuable skill, you will get ahead).

The differences between the American and British adolescents' beliefs may be attributed to a number of possible causes: the fact that youth unemployment is probably a more salient issue among British youth; more Americans go into higher education than do the British; there are fewer long-term provisions for the long-term unemployed in the USA than in Britain.

What is interesting about the items that most British adolescents either agreed or disagreed with (over 75 percent) was the fact that they were often naive and contradictory. Thus they believed in a welfare state (see item 10 agreed to by over 80 percent: It is the responsibility of the government to take care of people who can't take care of themselves) appeared to equally believe in free enterprise (e.g. item 42: Employers should have the right to hire non-union workers if they want to). It could, of course, be argued that in a mixed economy such as Britain these statements are not incompatible, yet the overall pattern of results (compare items 1 and 43) shows that the respondents do not follow clearly and unambiguously any one politicoeconomic line. Furthermore, the results seem also to indicate a relatively poor understanding of the workings of the economy as those items which require some understanding (e.g., 26: the role of saving) had a high percentage of uncertain responses.

The study also attempted to isolate those independent variables that best discriminated economic values. Very few (amount of pocket money received and political party preference vote) appeared to discriminate in logical patterns. This is in accordance with previous studies which have not found many clearly discriminating variables (Marshall and Magruder 1960; Furnham and Thomas 1984b). This may be due to the fact that the sample was drawn from a fairly homogeneous socioeconomic group. Indeed, O'Brien and Ingels (1985) found socioeconomic status one of their most discriminating independent variables (six out of eight factors yielded significant differences). However, whereas O'Brien and Ingels (1984) found vote (political party identification) did not discriminate with their sample (two out of eight factors showed significant differences), Furnham (1987) found vote the most discriminating variable (five out of eight factors showed significant differences). This may be due to the fact that in Britain, more than America, the political parties are divided on economic issues, and to a limited degree class (socioeconomic) differences. Furthermore, adolescents appear to be fairly interested, knowledgeable and aware of political issues in Britain (Furnham and Gunter 1983). It is also possible as Jahoda (1983) suggests that experience in the economy speeds up economic socialization and knowledge and that this may account for some of the difference between the two national groups.

Other studies related to young people's economic values concern their beliefs about how public expenditure should be decided. Lewis (1983) asked University student subjects first to estimate, then show preferences for public expenditure items. He found the subjects' political preferences clearly affected their preferences of what services public expenditure should be paid. Furnham (1987) replicated this finding on young people who were required to complete the *Public Expenditure* questionnaire devised by Lewis (1983). The questionnaire asks subjects to apportion the total annual budget (in terms of percentages) on seven macropublic expenditure items: Trade and Industry; Social Security; Defense; Education; Health and Welfare; Roads and Housing.

The results were fairly similar to the findings of Lewis (1983) save the fact that his student sample favored spending less on social security and more on education than this sample (12 vs. 17 per cent; 22 vs. 19 per cent). Interestingly the subjects appeared to want to spend most money on trade and industry, closely followed by health and welfare, and finally education.

Certainly, as Lewis (1983), has argued, public expenditure perceptions and preferences can be broadly predicted from social and political attitudes. Furnham (1987b) showed that not as many differences arise as in adults (Lewis 1983) but that predictable patterns do occur. It should be pointed out, however, that responses to his questionnaire may be relatively unstable as popular debate on such issues as defense strategy, social security (welfare) fraud, education cuts may significantly alter the response pattern of subjects. It is also questionable as to whether subjects know how much was currently spent by governments on the various budgets.

The two major public expenditure items that yielded consistent significant differences were (predictably) social security and defense. Whereas conservative voters believed that approximately equal amounts of revenue were, are and should be spent on each, leftwing labor supporters discriminated sharply between them favoring not unnaturally social welfare over defense. But what is perhaps most interesting is the way subjects of the left *and* right exaggerate the difference between expenditure on these two, underemphasizing the difference in their own preference. This may be seen as a sort of attribution error that may function to confirm one in one's own beliefs. Why this error does not extend to trade and industry (possibly favored by capitalistic conservatives) and health and welfare (possibly favored by socialist labor supporters) is unclear.

An advantage of asking people to estimate these public expenditure expenses is that one may compare their estimates with the actual sums spent on each item. By-and-large subjects were reasonably accurate but tended to *over*-estimate the amount spent on *defense* and *roads,* and underestimate the amount spent on *social security* and *education.* As Lewis (1983) noted in his study the results suggest that subjects from the "right" (Conservatives) tend to have a more accurate picture of public expenditure than subjects from the "left" (Labor).

Certainly the research on young people's economic values remains in its infancy but is both promising and interesting. More importantly, it may well be that the best predictor of economic behavior are economic values rather than economic knowledge. For those interested in economic education or political proselytizing the way in which economic values are developed and maintained is of significant interest and worthy of considerably more research.

## ECONOMIC SOCIALIZATION AND EDUCATION

If experiences in the home and marketplace can dramatically affect children's and adolescents' economic understanding, how are children formally and explicitly socialized by their parents and what are the effects of this? What experiences or what parental instructions make a difference? Why do parents and schools in western societies usually invest so little effort in economic instruction? Can formal, classroom-based economic education radically improve children's and adolescents' knowledge of the workings of the economy? What do people "pick-up" from the media which informs and shapes their economic understanding.

Work in this field falls into two major fields: work on pocket money and allowances as a means of studying how parents socialize the young into ways of using money, and effects of explicit teaching of some economic concepts. Stacey (1982) has divided the research on economic socialization into four different areas: money, possessions, social differentiation and inequality, and socioeconomic understanding. He concludes that most early experience of economic socialization appears to revolve around possessions which take on social characteristics. Between the ages of four and six, children seem to acquire monetary understanding by associating money with buying, but it is not until the age of about ten that the numerical value of money and the functional understanding of money transactions develop. At about the same time children begin to develop ideas of poverty, wealth, income, property and class differences. In early adolescence, teenagers are able to give near-adult explanations of economic events and relationships. Stacey (1982) concluded: "In the first decade of life, the economic socialization of children does not appear to be strongly influenced by their own social backgrounds, with the exception of the children to the very rich and possibly the very poor. In the second decade of life, social differences in the development appear to be more pronounced" (p. 172).

Perhaps the most important way in which parents from liberal democratic societies socialize their children in monetary and economic matters is through their pocket money (allowances)—a weekly or monthly allowance given either unconditionally or for some work. Almost no research has been done in this area although market research over an eight-year period in Britain has attempted to determine changes in pocket money patterns which naturally increase, roughly in line with inflation. Girls tended to get less than boys at all ages, and pocket money was often supplemented by part-time jobs, as well as gifts. It is also noted that children's spending power was almost £640 million a year on pocket money alone, and in addition £780 million in earnings from jobs and gifts from relatives are included (Walls 1983).

On the other hand, many popular articles have been written in an attempt to guide parents in the economic socialization of their children. Rarely, if ever, do they present data but are nearly always forceful, moralistic and middle class in their advice. Consider the following:

> The allowance should be paid weekly—on the same
> day of each week—to younger children, and monthly
> to kids as they approach their teens. The shift to
> monthly payment is not for your convenience but is
> for the purpose of encouraging more careful attention
> to budgeting and planning ahead on the part of your
> teenager. The important thing is that the payment
> should represent a predictable source of income that
> the child can count on. (Davis and Taylor 1979)

Fox (1978) has argued that, even by the time children
enter school, they already have experience in working, buying,
trading, owning, and saving. 'Research on children's informal
economic learning indicates that early economic instruction
in the classroom needs to take into account these unprocessed
experiences, economic attitudes and children's cognitive
capacities' (p. 137).

The study by Marshall and Magruder (1960) is one of the
few that specifically investigated the relationship between
parents' money education practices and children's knowledge
and use of money. Among the many hypotheses examined
were: 'children will have more knowledge of money use if
their parents give them an allowance' and 'children will have
more knowledge of the use of money if they save money'.
They found as predicted that children's knowledge of money
directly related to the extensiveness of their experience of
money—whether they are given money to spend, if they are
given opportunities to earn and save money and their parent's
attitudes to and habits of spending money. Thus it seems that
socialization and education would have important consequences on a child's or adolescent's understanding of
economic affairs. However, they did not find any evidence for
a number of their hypotheses. They were: children will have
more knowledge on money use if their parents give them an
allowance; if children are given allowances, less of the family's
money, rather than more, will be taken for children's

spending money; if children are given the opportunities to earn money, they will have more knowledge of money use than children lacking this experience; children will have less knowledge of money use if money is used to reward or punish their behavior; and children will have the attitudes about the importance of money and material things that are expressed by their parents.

In an extensive study of over 700 seven-year-olds, Newson and Newson (1976) found that most could count on a basic sum of pocket money, sometimes calculated on a complicated incentive system. Some children appear to be given more money for the express purpose of allowing the possibility of fining (confiscating); others are given it as a substitute for wages; while some have to work for it. Over 50 percent of the sample earned money from their parents beyond their regular income but there were no sex or social differences in their practice. They did, however, find occupational class differences in children's unearned income and savings. Middle class children received less (18 percent vs. 30 percent) than working-class children, and save more (90 percent vs 48 percent). That is, 52 percent of class V children (bottom of the socioeconomic scale) *always* spend their money within the week, whereas only 10 per cent of class I or II children do so (top of the socio-economic scale). The authors conclude:

> Having cash in hand is equated with enjoying the good life: the relationship between money and enjoyment is specific and direct... the working class child already begins to fall into this traditional pattern of life in the use of pocket money (p. 244).

Furnham and Thomas (1984b) set out to determine age, sex and class differences in the distribution and use of pocket money by testing over 400 7-12-year-old British children. Results showed there were many more age than sex or class differences in amounts received. Older children, not surprisingly, received more money, saved more, and were more likely to go shopping than younger children. Middle class children reported more than working class children that they had to work around the house for their pocket money and tended to let their parents look after the pocket money that they had saved. Overall, however, there were surprisingly few class differences, either because they no longer exist in Britain to the same extent as they did in the past or because the sample was unrepresentative in terms of classes from which the children were sampled or because class differences in economic behavior appear later in life.

More recently Furnham and Thomas (1984a) investigated adults' perceptions of the economic socialization of children through pocket money. Over 200 British adults completed a questionnaire on their beliefs concerning how much and how often children should be given pocket money, as well as such things as whether they should be encouraged to work for it, save it and so forth. The results indicated that females were more willing to treat children as responsible individuals, for instance, by negotiating the amount of money to be paid and the various duties that they would be expected to fulfil for it. Overall, as expected, middle class adults were more in favor of giving children money. Indeed, some working class respondents did not believe in the system of pocket money at all. A similar class difference was revealed with the question concerning when children should receive their pocket money. Whereas 91 percent of the middle class believed children should receive it weekly (and 4 percent thought when they need it) only 79 percent of working class adults believed children should receive their pocket money weekly (and 16 percent when they need it). Furthermore significantly more working class adults believed that boys should receive more pocket money than girls.

These class difference findings are in line with previous studies on childhood socialization (Newson and Newson 1976) and with figures on class differences in general. That is, working class adults introduce pocket money later and more erratically than middle class parents. However, the study of Furnham and Thomas (1984a) found far fewer class differences, which may be the result of the fact that a greater range of ages was considered in this study.

Certainly the research on pocket money allowances seems a most fruitful avenue of research, especially as so many researchers have reported that experience plays such an important part in the understanding of the economic world of children and adolescents. However, looking at economic socialization practices in different countries—socialist and capitalist, pre-industrial, industrial and post-industrial—may reveal equally important findings.

One of the more interesting applications of research on children's acquisition of economic concepts is the teaching of these concepts in school. For instance, there have been studies on the 'kinder-economy' or the 'mini-society' which involve classroom discussions of economic concepts like scarcity, opportunity cost, production, specialization, distribution, exchange and so on, followed by a long-term role play (Kourilsky & Campbell 1984). Kourilsky (1977) using 96, 5-6-year-olds attempted to answer four important questions: Is the child's success in economic decision making and analysis related to instructional intervention or to increased maturity inherent in the passage of time? To what extent and degree, through instructional intervention, are children able to master concepts that, psychologically, they are too young to learn? What type of school, home and personality variables are predictors of success in economic decision making and analysis? For example, does initiative predict success in economic decision making? What part is played by the parents in their day-to-day discussions with their child of his or her economic activities? What are the parents' attitudes toward the teaching of economic decision making and analytic principles as part of early childhood education?

Her results indicated that the children's understanding of economics was most strongly influenced by the intervention program even at an early age. From their answers, children appeared to be able to master concepts that developmentally they were considered too young to learn by that age. Yet the analysis showed that parental factors were the best predictors of economic mastery, more so than the cognitive, social or verbal development of the child. Finally, parents seemed very positive toward the intervention program, some even reporting that they found it embarrassing to find that their 5-year-olds knew more about economics than they did! Studies looking at the correlation between parents' and children's economic understanding might yield insights into how the socialization process works.

Certainly the widespread ignorance about economics in children, adolescents and adults suggests the importance and relevance of beginning to teach the subject even in junior/primary school. There are also practical reasons for teaching economics principles. First, adolescents have considerable buying power, for instance, and it is of considerable interest to people in trade to know how, where and why that money is spent. Second, teachers of economics are clearly interested in the way economic concepts are acquired so that they may teach them more effectively at the appropriate age (Kourilsky 1977; O'Brien and Ingels 1985). Indeed, there is a *Journal of Economic Education* dedicated specifically to research into the teaching of economics. There are many interesting theoretical questions concerning adolescents' understanding and beliefs about the economy, such as at what age various sophisticated economic concepts are grasped, gender differences in economic beliefs and attitudes, the effectiveness of teaching by using role plays or 'mini-economies', etcetera. More importantly perhaps it could be argued that only if people understand the principles and benefits of the capitalist, free-market system can they be induced to vote for it.

Economic socialization occurs in three ways: parental instruction and practices (i.e., giving pocket money); formal schooling in economics and related topics (politics, sociology, accountancy); and personal experience of the economy by personal shopping, work experience, attention to advertising on the mass media, etcetera. Clearly all three are important but are very difficult to separate. What the results in this area indicate is that, although economic beliefs and understanding appear to develop in systematic stages, the speed of changes as well as the end-point of development can be substantially modified by primary, secondary or tertiary socialization.

## CONCLUSION

The literature on child and adolescent understanding of the economic world is highly diffuse and of varying empirical quality. Most of the research has attempted to describe the stages of understanding in a developmental sequence. There is, however, a good deal of disagreement about the number of stages, the points of transition and the exact nature of the understanding in each stage. Considerably less work has gone into describing those factors which speed up or slow down the transition from one stage to another or individual differences within the various stages. Social class, exposure to the economic world, parental practices and formal teaching seem the most important determinants of children's economic knowledge and use of money, though there may well be other important determinants, such as their schooling experiences, the amount and type of economic activity in the town or country where they live and perhaps most importantly, the economic and political regime in which they live. The importance of this area cannot be underestimated as it seems possible that habits of using money (spending, saving, gambling, etc.) are established in childhood or at least early adolescence.

Current research in this area has tended to focus on an issue of current concern, namely unemployment (Furnham

1985b). For instance, studies have looked at schoolchildren's ideas about how to get a job (Furnham 1984a) as well as their concepts of unemployment (Webley and Wrigley 1983). Indeed, it is this lack of programmatic research into economic socialization and development that probably accounts for the comparative paucity of real findings in this area. Although there is some consensus in the results from very different studies in this area, many critical questions remain about children's and adolescents' knowledge of the economic world.

Lea (et al. 1987) have made a number of important points regarding the research on young people's economic understanding. First, is that studies that have concentrated too much on cognitive structure and stages of thought have tended to underemphasize the very important roles of content and context in shaping understanding. That is, they do not attempt to analyze or describe how, when and where significant aspects of the child's environment contribute to their understanding. Second, that economic understanding is intimately linked to political understanding and the grasping of constructs like power, equality and the nature of ideology. Consequently, they stress the role of schools, media advertising and parents in the socialization of various economic beliefs and behaviors. They note: "...we should examine the economic world that children are constructing themselves. Bartering, swapping, allocating roles (e.g. in games) and rewards, giving presents to teachers and friends, betting and daring, are all activities that deserve our attention... The more we learn about the autonomous economic world of childhood, the more developmental economic psychology will be able to inform us about the influence of the economy on the individuals who live within it and the way in which those individuals in turn shape economic structure" (pp. 398-399).

Finally, the political implications of this research cannot be over-emphasized. A young person's understanding of how the economy functions no doubt can and does influence their everyday behavior. Important decisions like which job to apply for; whether to attempt house purchasing; saving; and which political party to vote for are probably a direct function of economic understanding and values. Any group working to promote adherence to a political philosophy, whether it be socialist, capitalist or some mix, would do well to concentrate some effort influencing young peoples' understanding.

# REFERENCES

Berti, A., & Bombi, A. (1979). Where does money come from? *Archivio di Psycologia, 40,* 53-77.

Berti, A., & Bombi, A. (1981). The development of the concept of money and its value: A longitudinal study. *Child Development, 52,* 1179-1182.

Berti, A., Bombi, A., & Lis, A. (1982). The child's conception about means of production and their owners. *European Journal of Social Psychology, 12,* 221-239.

Berti, A., Bombi, A., & de Bein, R. (1986). The development of economic notions: Single sequence and separate acquisitions. *Journal of Economic Psychology, 7,* 415-424.

Brown, L. & Lalljee, M. (1981). Young persons' conceptions of criminal events. *Journal of Moral Education, 10,* 105-112.

Burris, V. (1983). Stages in the development of economic concepts. *Human Relations, 9,* 791-812.

Cummings, S., & Taebel, V. (1978). The economic socialization of children: A neo-Marxist analysis. *Social Problems, 26,* 198-210.

Damon, W. (1977). *The Social World of the Child.* San Francisco: Jossey-Bass.

Danziger, K. (1958). Children's earliest conception of economic relationships. *Journal of Social Psychology, 47,* 231-240.

Davis, K., & Taylor, T. (1979). *Kids and Cash: Solving a Parent's Dilemma*. La Jolla: Oak Tree.

Fox, K. (1978). What children bring to school: The beginning of economic education. *Social Education, 10,* 478-481.

Furby, L. (1978). Possessions: Toward a theory of their meaning and function throughout the life cycle. In P. Baltes (ed.), *Life-span Development and Behaviour* (Vol.1). New York: Academic Press.

Furby, L. (1979). Inequalities in personal possessions: Explanations for and judgments about unequal distribution. *Human Development, 22,* 180-202.

Furby, L. (1980). The origins and early development of possessive behaviour. Political Psychology, 2, 30-42.

Furnham, A. (1982a). The perception of poverty among adolescents. *Journal of Adolescence, 5,* 135-147.

Furnham, A. (1982b). Why are the poor always with us? Explanations of poverty in Britain. *British Journal of Social Psychology, 21,* 311-322.

Furnham, A. (1984a). Getting a job—school leavers perceptions of employment prospects. *British Journal of Educational Psychology, 54,* 293-305.

Furnham, A. (1984b). The protestant work ethic: A review of the psychological literature. *European Journal of Social Psychology, 14,* 87-104.

Furnham, A. (1985). Youth unemployment: A review of the literature. *Journal of Adolecence, 8,* 109-124.

Furnham, A. (1989). The determinants and structure of adolescent's beliefs about the economy. *Journal of Economic Psychology, 12,* 353-371.

Furnham, A., & Cleare, A. (1986). School children's conceptions of economics: Price, wages, investments and strikes. *Journal of Economic Psychology.*

Furnham, A., & Jones, S. (1987). Children's view regarding possessions and their theft. *Journal of Moral Education, 16,* 18-30.

Furnham, A., & Lewis, A. (1986). *The Economic Mind: The Social Psychology of Economic Behaviour.* Brighton, Sx: St. Martin.

Furnham, A., & Stacey, B. (1990). *Young People's Understanding of Society.* London: Routledge.

Furnham, A., & Thomas, P. (1984a). Adults' perception of the economic socialization of children. *Journal of Adolescence, 7,* 217-231.

Furnham, A., & Thomas, P. (1984b). Pocket money: A study of economic education. *British Journal of Developmental Psychology, 2,* 205-212.

Furth, H. (1980). *The World of Grown-ups.* New York: Elsevier.

Ingels, S., & O'Brien, M. (1985). An evaluation of the impact on attitudes and values of the text. In *Our Economy.* Chicago: University of Chicago.

Irving, K., & Siegal, M. (1983). Mitigating circumstances in children's perceptions of criminal justice. *British Journal of Developmental Psychology, 1,* 179-188.

Jahoda, G. (1979). The construction of economic reality by some Glaswegian children. *European Journal of Social Psychology, 9,* 115-127.

Jahoda, G. (1981). The development of thinking about economic institution: The bank. *Cahiers de Psychologie Cognitive, 1,* 55-78.

Jahoda, G. (1983). European 'lay' in the development of an economic concept: A study in Zimbabwe. *British Journal of Developmental Psychology, 1,* 110-120.

Jahoda, G., & Woerdenbagch, A. (1982). The development of ideas about economic institution: A cross-national replication. *British Journal of Social Psychology, 21,* 337-338.

Kourilsky, M. (1977). The kinder-economy: A case study of kindergarten pupils' acquisition of economic concepts. *Elementary School Journal, 77,* 182-191.

Kourilsky, M., & Campbell, M. (1984). Sex differences in a simulated classroom economy: Children's beliefs about entrepreneurship. *Sex Roles, 10,* 53-66.

Lea, S., Tarpy, R., & Webley, P. (1987). The Individual in the Economy. Cambridge: Cambridge University Press.

Leahy, R. (1981). The development of the conception of economic inequality: Descriptions and comparisons of rich and poor people. *Child Development, 52,* 523-532.

Leiser, D. (1983). Children's conceptions of economics: The constitution of a cognitive domain. *Journal of Economic Psychology, 4,* 297-317.

Lewis, A. (1983). Public expenditure: Perceptions and preferences. *Journal of Economic Psychology, 3,* 159-167.

Marshall, H., & Magruder, L. (1960). Relations between parent money education practices and children's knowledge and use of money. *Child Development, 31,* 253-284.

McGrew, W. (1972). *An Ethological Study of Children's Behaviour.* New York: Academic Press.

McNeal, J. (1987). *Children as Consumers: Insights and Implications.* Lexington: Lexington Books.

Miller, L., & Horn, T. (1955). Children's concepts regarding debt. *Elementary School Journal, 56,* 406-412.

Newson, J., & Newson, E. (1976). *Seven Year-olds in the Home Environment.* London: George Allen and Unwin.

Ng, S. (1983). Children's ideas about the bank and shop prefit: Development stages and the influence of cognitive contrasts and conflict. *Journal of Economic Psychology, 4,* 209-221.

O'Brien, M., & Ingels, S. (1984). *The Development of the Economic Values Inventory.* Chicago: University of Chicago Press.

O'Brien, M., & Ingels, S. (1987). The economic values inventory. *Research in Economic Education, 18,* 7-18.

Patterson, J., & Locksley, G. (1981). How fifth formers see the unions. *Labour Research, 11,* 23-25.

Pollis, H., & Gray, T. (1973). Change-making strategies in children and adults. *Journal of Psychology, 84,* 173-179.

Sevón, G., and Weckstrom, S. (1989). The development of reasoning about economic events: A study of Finnish children. *Journal of Economic Psychology, 10,* 495-514.

Siegal, M. (1981). Children's perception of adult economic needs. *Child Development, 52,* 379-382.

Siegal, M., & Shwalb, D. (1985). Economic justice in adolescence: An Australian-Japanese comparison. *Journal of Economic Psychology, 6,* 313-326.

Stacey, B. (1982). Economic socialization in the pre-adult years. *British Journal of Social Psychology, 21,* 159-173.

Strauss, A. (1952). The development and transformation of monetary meanings in the child. *American Sociological Review, 17,* 275-286.

Sutton, R. (1962). Behaviour in the attainment of economic concepts. *Journal of Psychology, 53,* 37-46.

Tan, H., & Stacey, B. (1981). The understudy of socio-economic concepts in Malaysian Chinese school children. *Child Study Journal, 11,* 33-49.

Waines, N. (1984). Development of economic concepts among Egyptian children. *Journal of Cross-Cultural Psychology, 15,* 49-54.

Walls Ltd. (1983). *Pocket Money Monitor.* Surrey: Birds Eye, Walls Ltd.

Webley, P., & Wrigley, V. (1983). The development of conceptions of unemployment among adolescents. *Journal of Adolescence, 6,* 317-320.

Winocur, S., & Siegal, M. (1982). Adolescents' judgements of economic arrangements. *International Journal of Behavioural Development, 5,* 357-365.

Witryol, S., & Wentworth, N. (1983). A paired comparison scale of children's preference for monetary and material rewards used in investigations of incentive effects. *Journal of Genetic Psychology, 142,* 17-23.

# WORK AND EMPLOYMENT

# CHAPTER 9

# HUMAN CAPITAL AND SOCIAL STRATIFICATION

*Dennis O'Keeffe*

This chapter is in two parts. In the first, I argue that modern capitalist society has a unique class-structure, given mainly by human capital formation. Such a society is characterized by an unprecedented openness and by a degree of integrative consensus unthinkable in any previous large-scale society, and not to be found in what remains of the contemporary socialist world. In the second part, I suggest that in the case of British society, this wholly beneficial development is threatened and compromised by the strange pathology of modern British education, of which I offer a tentative analysis. The reference is mainly British; but the intention is to say something general about the socioeconomy of modern liberal society.

## THE DARLINGS OF HISTORY:
## THE HUMAN CAPITAL ORDER

One of the theoretical commonplaces of sociology used to be that in the recent past the system of social stratification of the advanced societies had moved from "ascription" to "achievement." People were increasingly graded socially on the grounds of their activities and less and less on the basis of the intractable, caste-like features of social inheritance. The rewards of success, such as high income, the accumulation of wealth and the receipt of prestige from fellow citizens, no longer resided in one's name and connections: now it was to be a man's *actions* which determined his place in the world. Such, at any rate, was the general ambience of American functionalist sociology in the 1940s and 1950s.

On the face of it, this theoretical approach had obvious appeal. It was a telling historical apercu, in a sociological oeuvre whose main disadvantage, I shall argue, was its lack of historical purchase. It described one society—the USA—pretty well after all; and though Great Britain and France, etcetera, lagged behind the USA in this matter, it seemed very probable that where America led other societies would in due time follow. And why not? The theoretical model, closely associated with its American exemplar, had great and compelling attractions. Capitalist America had acquired, during the nineteenth century, a reputation which she has ever since retained, more or less intact, as an open and meritocratic society, where the accidents of birth counted less than the deliberate demonstration of ability. Even America's image in modern neo-Marxist mythology, as the *fons et origo* of the world's ills, is only an impoverished inversion of the historical truth.[1] That truth is that the capitalist economic system is the only one, so far, that seems able to permit large numbers of people to live in relative security and dignity.

Now that the "capitalist phenomenon" is spreading, apparently inexorably, across the face of the globe, its socialist rival in hopeless disarray and decline, it is important that we do not neglect the historical achievements of the Anglo-Saxons. Such a neglect comes easily to modern sociologists, with their ignorance of history and economics. The etiology of the market-system is a complex one;[2] but a sketch history of this extraordinary success story presents few problems. Where the British contribution had been to lift a society, for the first time, out of the intractable horrors of agrarianism, America had gone further, her development by World War II defying, as Mr. Potter has so aptly put it, "even Texan superlatives."[3]

It was the novelty, unpredictability and suddenness of capitalism which the sociologists seemed to find difficult to grasp. The functionalist model, for all its theoretical optimism and generosity, was in some ways deficient, we now see. It lacked historical perspective.[4] Though the idea of a shift from ascription to achievement did gain a hold, this was about the limit of historical sophistication in the functionalist paradigm. This neglect of the extraordinary historical originality of modern capitalist society was what was later to leave theoretical sociology helpless in the face of the neo-Marxist challenge. The Marxists had a wrong history; functionalism had none at all. Its proponents mistook the particularities of genius in the system it explained, as universals, falsely attributing a comparable importance to integrative consensus in other societies.[5] The critical inadequacy of the twentieth century sociology of capitalism has been its failure to identify the *specifically capitalist* character and historical originality, in societies such as ours, of the processes of socialization, social control and consensus.

It is important, but not enough to rebut the neo-Marxist critique of consensus as "false consciousness," "misrecognition" or "repressive tolerance."[6] These absurd and debased latter-day Platonisms are the very stuff of contemporary Marxian condescension. The myth of the alienated and manipulated proletarian or "mass-cultural" puppet, suspended on bourgeois strings, is the most grotesque and patronizing one in the whole of the contemporary "radical" armory.

We should have gone on the attack. Our social control is not repressive; it is based on rational, internalized approval. The bourgeois and the proletarian are not enemies but allies. And their secular contacts, within an increasingly sophisticated division of labor, direct the worker into increasingly middle class aspirations and mores. The classic prole is increasingly marginalized—a creature of technological retardation. The new proles, the welfariat, are the products of social engineering and 1960's morality. They correspond more to what Marx himself despised as a *lumpenproletariat.*

Out in the real world the capitalist engine of unplanned prosperity moves on, history's most striking example to-date of beneficial serendipity. No one could have conceived, much less planned it[7] Therein lies its genuine character. The consensus is genuine. People like earning their own incomes, making their own economic decisions, owning their own houses and cars. They learn and approve the rules. Industrialization has indeed been a move from ascription to achievement. It has also been a move from *coercion to consensus.* There has occurred a dramatic transformation in the principles of social control. The precarious influence of coercion has been replaced by an historically unprecedented consensus. In a capitalist economy, an increasing part of social life comes to be regulated by the principles of the *market.* Yet the sociologists continue to speak in the language of class warfare. In a society in which untranscendable accidents of birth are of less significance than they have ever been, a writer like Basil Bernstein still feels obliged to identify class as "the dominant cultural category" of capitalism.[8]

There could scarcely be a more signal error. Class, in fact, is in capitalist society only a derivative phenomenon in the main. It is in process of endless deconstruction and reconstitution. Only the mildest of residual ascription informs our social hierarchy. The true key is the set of arrangements, provisional and impersonal, which arise from the ever-changing division of labor, and its motor: knowledge and technology. There is a crude truth, therefore, in the British Registrar General's occupational categories. It is the work which one does which settles, in the main, one's place in the social world. And no generation in the past has been as free in its work choices as we, none less bound in them by the work its parents did. The division of labor has made of us the darlings of history.

This needs some spelling out. I contend that the main framework for social hierarchy in our kind of society is the job-structure, to which people relate differentially in terms of their differing accumulations of human capital. To put a complex matter rather simply, human capital is the extra earning power formed in people by education and training, health maintenance and migration. Education is the biggest factor–in all societies for which we have the requisite data, educated people earn more than less educated people, on average.[9] This is one of the great empirical findings of modern social science, the question being not *whether* but *why* it is so. In any case, whatever might account for the education/earnings nexus, it remains a fact that the possession of *bona fide* educational credentials constitutes an undeniable capital.[10]

Nor are the benefits of such a capital confined to income differentials. Though the matter has been much less closely researched, human capital formation is also intimately linked to the distribution of status.[11] The "human capital order" should have been the explanatory focus of economic sociology for a couple of decades by now. Alas, sociologists have preferred the onanistic fastnesses of neo-Marxism! Whatever explanatory purchase the Marxian socioeconomy of private property may once have possessed, however, it possesses it no longer.

Why should an illuminating economic sociology or "socioeconomy" as I prefer to call it, have been so slow to appear? Sad to say, sociology has proved itself as comprehensively ill-informed about economics as about history. The fact is, economics and sociology have, unjustifiably, refused to continue that partnership which looked so promising in the work of Max Weber.[12] True, there are faults on both sides. The modern story of economics is not entirely a happy one. We live in the mess created by Keynesian-statism. The corporate state is a vast and deeply entrenched monument to past errors in economic reasoning. But sociology has been far worse than economics. The kind of gentle ridicule I have occasionally endured at the hands of a market-minded economist like Arthur Seldon[13] has been thoroughly deserved by most of my sociological colleagues. The fanatical egalitarianism of modern British sociology typifies that of the intelligentsia as a whole. Indeed, sociologists have been the principal conduits for this strange and unrealizable persuasion. If governments had listened wholeheartedly to them, we would not just have a third-rate education system to contend with: we would be in the Third World.

In recent years, sociologists have tended to discredit their discipline by an astonishing neglect of key issues like markets and scarcity, combined with a naive and sentimental socialism. In sum, economics and sociology have grown apart in modern scholarship, and our unhappy sociology of today reflects that separation. Sociologists have been able to misconstrue society because they have not understood economy.

I know of no major work in modern sociology, for example, which seems able to reconcile the coexistence of economic impersonality, the neutral laws of the market, with functional integrative consensus, indeed consensus of historically novel power and coherence. Yet the two coexist: depersonalized economic agents and a very lightly enforced social structure. Indeed, it is this coexistence which explains why this is the first society since the Stone Age which does not resort to terrible coercion and violence as part of its standard system of control. The market economy does not transcend scarcity–no economy ever will—but it greatly alleviates it. Pre-industrial economies were characterized by an inflexible supply of resources, which in turn, imparted a grimly zero-sum character to their social arrangements. Capitalism has proved itself not, as the Marxists held, the supreme and most intense expression of class warfare, but the means for its abolition.

# HUMAN CAPITAL AND SOCIAL STRATIFICATION

The functionalist sociologists did not recognize the debt which the society they studied owed to the capitalist economy. They celebrated the system without grasping its specifically capitalist character. This failure laid the way open for the neo-Marxists of the 1960s and 1970s and their identification of capitalism as the source of, rather than the solution to, the recurring economic dilemmas of our race.[14] Not hostile to capitalism, the functionalist sociologists failed, nevertheless, to build up comparative models which might have revealed its historical novelty, which might have revealed its explanatory power as an idea and its productive power as a system.

The most remarkable phenomenon of all about modern capitalism is its powers of social legitimation. These relate specifically to all the features which Marx attacked: the division of labor, private property, money wages. The operational condition for all these is a free labor market wherein men and women can invest inalienably in themselves, and accumulate living human capital. We can now see that in slave or feudal societies there is no comparable apparatus of socialization through which a genuine participating citizenry which both has, and believes itself to have, a real stake in the social order, can emerge. Moreover, we are now in a position to see that modern communism, at least in terms of social control and stratification, has far more in common with the various forms of agrarian society than either communism or agrarianism have with modern capitalism.

Modern communism has been a dichotomous system of stratification, relying on periodic or underlying violence for the securing of control. Whatever its historical novelty as a self-propelled engine of chaos and despotism, it is at least in its attachment to cruelty and violence an atavism, the reclothing of the ancient slave-state in the preposterous garb of modern pseudo-science.[15] The last few years have shown clearly how heavily socialist society always rested on coercion, and how feeble, whatever psychological disfigurements it may have visited on its unfortunate denizens, its apparatus of socialization and legitimacy has been. Communism now stands revealed as unmistakably burdened with seemingly insoluble problems of legitimation. Not only is its economic performance derisory; it has created a sullen and alienated denizenry, inert and suspicious. This mentality is the worst problem the post-communist world faces in its attempts at reconstruction.

## THE DICHOTOMOUS MODEL OF STRATIFICATION

Most of the societies of recorded history have been essentially, dichotomously stratified. There were many sorts of marginal strata in these societies. There were many *differences* between these various societies. But they all had in common a basic pattern. In all of them there were fundamentally two, and only two, strata or classes. The majority were slaves, serfs or peasants. The minority were slave-owners or slave-controllers, nobility or gentry.

I am not suggesting sufficient overlap between the various forms of slavery, feudalism and "early" modern society, to justify an overarching term. This is the mistake made by Wittfogel with his "Oriental Despotism."[16] Such a term is meritricious. It unites unbridgeably different societies within a common taxonomy. I am suggesting nothing so ambitious, or putting it pejoratively, promiscuous. And my collection of societies is neither as large nor as motley as Wittfogel's. What I *am* suggesting is that the different forms of large-scale agrarian society have, for all their differences, certain irreducible features in common.

## THE PARADOXES OF THE MARXIST CRITIQUE

The central paradox of Marxist praxis, is that having wrongly identified capitalist society as a dichotomous system of stratification, its own curative prospectus, once enacted, produces precisely such a two-tone stratification. The division between nomenklatura and the rest is sharper and more definitive than any known to free enterprise systems.[17] Marx is well-known to have identified the evils of capitalism in the single phrase "private property." This is an example of the intellectual inflation of a lesser, though not insignificant truth, at the expense of a much more significant one. That lesser truth, in any case, concerns wealth not capitalism. It is true that wealth is a source of position and power. Even as we admit this, however, we shall surely stress that such a view dangerously obscures a far more important truth: namely that wealth is also a source of human liberation.

As for the rest of the critique of estrangement/alienation—it is virtually worthless, the truths it contains quite overwhelmed by its errors. The division of labor may bring some narrow specialism, some adverse and deadening psychological effects on human beings. Its overthrow will bring mass famine. Money transactions may, human nature being what it is, result in frantic materialism on the part of some people. But to overstress this is to damn a system for its incidental malfeatures. Look at the more than 70 years in which the Soviets tried to suppress the money-transactions economy! As for money wages, I shall maintain in this essay that the supreme gift of capitalist society is its equipping of individuals with human capital.

Above all, private property, human capital, the division of labor and general money transactions, supply the main agency of economic socialization in modern capitalist society. Citizens learn an elaborate "market code" of buying, selling, consuming, investing and saving which is both functional to their coping in the modern economy, and also attaches them to the existing social order. Access to these key patterns of economic decision-making is given by the accumulation of *human capital* which is the true capital of modern capitalist society, or anyway just as indispensable as physical capital. The Marxist treatment of capital and labor as discrete, homogeneous variables, should not be subjected to a naive attack. It is the purest nineteenth century orthodoxy. All nineteenth century economics made the same period error.

But Marx brought into his analysis certain auxiliary material–from which Marxist "sociology" is mostly derived–which is wrong even in its own contemporary terms. Most notable among its faults from our specific point of view has been its utter failure to predict and explain the nature of social stratification in societies such as ours.

The theory of exploitation is hopeless. Either it merely confuses poverty and exploitation, or it smuggles a normative term into an analysis affecting scientific status. The idea that poverty as such constitutes exploitation is one which Marx both employs and judiciously denies. As Antony Flew observes, Marx dropped the time-series of British wages when it failed to confirm his immiseration thesis.[18] The false equation of poverty with exploitation remains, however, the most potent element in the revolutionary prospectus, and a mechanical assumption in sociological texts. We are lucky in countries like Britain, where this envious error imprisons only a few million members of the welfariat. In much of the Third World, such ideas are the root inspiration for the destitution of countless millions of souls.

As for the attempt, via the theory of surplus value extraction, to give scientific respectability to exploitation—it was never more than verbal trickery, in which no one of any reputation any longer believes. We have known for ages that in competitive markets, earnings tend to settle at the level of marginal productivity. In a free labor-market the bourgeois cannot, by definition, exploit the proletarian, who will simply move to alternative employment if any such attempt is made.

Where social stratification in the agrarian societies had been sharp and dichotomous, in the main unbridgeable, indeed upheld by ascriptive ideology and–more important–by violence, stratification in capitalist societies is fluid, gradualist and multifaceted. Overall, the system is characterized by upward social mobility, the gradual and apparently irreversible movement of most people to a "middle-class" position. This tendency has more to do with the spontaneous evolution of the capitalist economy than with deliberate attempts at social engineering. There are many paths of ascent, independent or overlapping; and without question "convergence" seems the most appropriate noun to describe the process. This gradual, fluid and provisional character of social hierarchy in our society explains its great advantages in the matter of self-legitimation compared to its agrarian predecessors and its modern communist alternative. The minority beneficiaries of such dichotomous structures have great difficulties in legitimating the social order. In capitalist society there is simply no such dichotomy to be justified.

## MISANTHROPY VS. MARKETS: THE CHALLENGE OF EDUCATIONAL SOCIALISM

The tendency for our society to transcend the ancient hatreds and grudges of history was first observed years ago. Indeed, it was even admitted by mild socialists like Anthony Crosland.[19] Academic sociologists since, committed class-warriors, have chosen for their obscurantist purposes to deny that it is happening. Socialist intellectuals have both wrongly explained and adversely influenced social stratification and social mobility. They also wrongly named the process which they denied was happening. They called it "embourgeoisement" and thereby introduced to English usage the correct French conflation of the middle class and the bourgeois.

The more recent record of British sociology is scarcely better. The sour egalitarianism of Halsey or Goldthorpe permits them only the most oblique and grudging acknowledgement of the extraordinary mass success story which their data reveal.[20] We cannot understand the difficulties without understanding the curious mutation in "educated" thought which has occurred in the Western societies in recent decades. It has manifested itself as an amorphous and shambling phenomenon, but nonetheless threatening for that. It celebrates the person and his rights but deprecates individual responsibilities, in effect, delegating them to the state. It is deeply antinomian and self-doubting. It dismisses or invades and distorts religion. It castigates males, whites and police, as well as big business. It repudiates traditional patriotism and yet it rejoices in transferred nationalisms. It rejects long-established cultural enthusiasms and yet it pursues an intellectually flatulent and lifeless multiculturalism, whose only real energy is displayed in its relentless persecution of non-conformists and its creation of jobs for the persons.[21]

Its central ideas have been class and class-warfare. Now, of course, these themes are on "hold." Increasingly, as these ideas have been exposed as falsehoods, their exponents, without ever admitting their persistent error, have latched onto new "injustices of stratification"—in particular those of race, sex and culture. What causes this self-doubt I do not know; probably it has to do with the decline in religious belief. In any event, not since the seventeenth century has so bizarre a pattern of malice and naivete held any kind of sway in this country. It is as weird and ostensibly unlikely an accompaniment to modern rationalism as the witchcraft craze was to the Renaissance. If ever one wanted a demonstration of Hayek's "fatal conceit" then surely this is it. The huge "planned" Robbins-sanctioned expansion of higher education has come to this: there are hundreds of thousands of men and women who have passed through the system, and instead of the humane skepticism that an enlightened society should expect, we find among the intellectuals a baroque credulity.

In the population at large, by contrast, we find far lower educational standards than are consistent with the proper requirements of a market economy. The great and the good in this country have not given enough attention to education outside the more prestigious schools and universities. Indeed, the word "neglect" springs immediately to mind. The education of many of the British has been neglected. Neglect of standards has been characteristic of socialist societies in the twentieth century; but what is true of the socialism of whole societies can also be true of the sectoral socialism of non-socialist ones. The underlying theoretical argument of this chapter, is that the essential problem of our education is that we persist in trying to combine a market-economy with a socialist education-system.

The similarity between general and educational socialism also extends to faults of commission. In both cases, voracious egalitarianism has been at work. The schools of this country have been the site of a protracted attempt at social, indeed, socialist engineering. This corresponds to rather little in the market economy, or in the political or everyday lives of most citizens. What it does is to compound the effects of negligence. In sum, the socioeconomic principles which regulate the education system are different from those which prevail in the wider society.

## EDUCATION AS AN UNCHARTED WILDERNESS

There is another crucial aspect of our education system which establishes its socialist credentials. It is surely not stuffy and old-fashioned to believe that education, of all ideas and activities, is the one most closely associated with information, facts and data. These are integral to the pursuit of knowledge. The truth, however, is that in this respect, we are in massive deficit. And that deficit is a classic example of socialism, it being almost a law of socialism that it suppresses the data needed for informational profiles, either indefinitely or, as in modern Russia, until the system has entered terminal paralysis. The British curriculum is like a mild, writ-small version of an old East European economy. We do not command enough information. In particular, the officially commissioned and garnered information we have about the output of the system is hopelessly inadequate.[22] The map of standards and achievement is scandalously incomplete. All the same, we do have some data to back up what anyone who is not blind can see for himself. There is, for example, the work of the never to be too much praised Office of Adult Literacy and Basic Skills Unit.[23]

In summary form, the findings of this unit are that in the post-school population; there is 10 percent functional illiteracy and 10 percent functional innumeracy and a 14 percent overlap of the two, using very modest criteria as to what counts as literate and numerate. The question is not *whether* but *why* this is so. That there are many causes which must be at work is scarcely in dispute. Television, divorce, the one-parent family—all these must be playing a part; but it is inconceivable to me that school and college have no part to play.

It should also be said that knowledge of literacy and numeracy does other work of an implicit kind for us. Illiteracy and innumeracy by near definition imply poor knowledge of science, technology, art, culture and so on. The relationship is not mechanical; there could be technological, musical or artistic geniuses who are unable to read, write or calculate. We may safely assume, however, that their numbers are small. They are like the intellectually gifted child-writer who cannot spell and does not know syntax. In other words, they are an abstract blend of sentimentality and special pleading.

## EDUCATION AS A PATHOLOGY

The pathological potential of mass education systems was another problem overlooked by functionalist sociology. We can see now that this blend of theorizing was tied in with a mechanistic, and far too optimistic, view of long-run cultural transmission in societies like ours. Another way of putting this would be to say that there was a failure to predict—or perhaps read off from the past—the role of intellectual misanthropy in modern civilization.

What I contend is that my country today is gripped by an enormous and terrifying intellectual crisis. In the USA, things are probably worse. The crisis has huge economic implications. If left unattended it could lead to the abortion of our attempts at an economic renaissance. Less obviously, the crisis has a kind of economic genesis. It is a function of a certain socioeconomic organization. It is a product of a socialistic removal of the major business of educating the nation's young people from all the sobering influence of the citizenry. Socialism is an economic system predicated on precisely this exclusion. Since I do not want to be misunderstood, I must stress that I am not here proposing the reduction of education to economics. The basic and ultimate language of education is philosophy. Nevertheless, the destruction of education has been mediated by the same collectivist phenomenon which has ruined half of the world's economic life.[23]

The family likeness between totalitarian socialism and the educational socialism of Western societies is apparent here. Bolsheviks had faith but no evidence that their way would lead to the betterment of the human race. They came to their engagement with destiny, armed with a massive misunderstanding of the modern world and its recent history. Just so with the egalitarians of the curriculum in countries like Great Britain and the United States. They have no easy way of showing who are the needy of the curriculum and why. They seem to have got it wrong whatever their good intentions.

At times, it is hard to accept that intentions are good anyway. Certainly, I find the idea of worrying little children about what color they are, etcetera, grotesque in the extreme. No matter, the self-appointed guardians of equality will act as their voice, and as the voice of downtrodden femininity, even if the grounds of this various downtroddenness seem hard to specify and remain obstinately unregistered in the innocent consciousness of childhood.

In fact, in the education system as a whole, politics has triumphed over economics. Instead of economic democracy we have political elitism. Worse, the discredited system of bureaucratic centralism—Lenin's malevolent gift to posterity—has come to dominate the regulation of learning and scholarship. Why should so important a part of the economic system as education have shown itself so given to secrecy, closure and remote and insolent managerialism? Now finally, in the birthplace of the Common Law, education is moving toward a version of the political corporate state, with not more than a few points of economic "exit" by way of compensation. Why should education, so crucial a manifestation of the division of labor, assume these grotesque, corporatist and socialist tendencies? Are those who say that every civilization has its immanent nemesis correct? Perhaps there is behind every great culture a sinister doppelgänger, counting off its numbered days. Sometimes one is almost physically aware of that mocking laughter somewhere just offstage, scorning our achievements, warming our enemies, intent on the spreading of misanthropy and despair.

The overall "progressive" package contains, in fact, two principal intellectual components locked together mainly by a preemptive foreclosing of questions. The former is the Rousseau-Dewey emphasis on the moral goodness, self-propelled educability and overriding psychological needs of the individual child. The second, which also derives more from Rousseau than from any other identifiable source, is the general disparagement of civilization, the cultivation of misanthropy. David Levy has usefully called the theoretical manifestation of this strange disposition "the hermeneutics of suspicion."[25] In the especially trite and tedious version which laborers in teacher-education's vineyard have predictably constructed, there is a set of adverse markers to be ranged against the moral perfection of childhood—ethnocentrism, sexism and racism being the main ones. If we translate this into a less ugly terminology, we still run up against a horrid antipathy in which Great Britain, men and white people are all to be objects of the greatest suspicion.

Why anyone should want to believe these strange things remains one of our greatest modern mysteries. It was Joseph Schumpeter, who long ago, pointed out that modern civilization seems to generate intellectual misanthropy. Indeed, he added that it actually rewards it.[26] What has never been satisfactorily explained is why misanthropy and antinomianism should be attractive in the first place. Nor did

Schumpeter, whose own work continued to drip with Marxist nostalgia, explain why it is publicly financed activities which most encourage the "radical" temper. Indeed, he seems not to have noticed that such is the case. The link between the two seems to me to warrant profound research and reflection.

David Marsland, who has long striven to create an intellectually respectable sociology, demonstrates in *Seeds of Bankruptcy* the deplorable and propagandist socialist bias in modern academic sociology.[27] I contend that a milder version of this same bias is at work in the education system as a whole. It is milder in the sense that it is vaguely socialist rather than specifically Marxist. The family likeness is given by the closing off of options, the pre-emption of the intellectual agenda. Having charted this intellectual pathology in some degree, however sketchily, it now behooves me to suggest some of its effects vis-à-vis social stratification.

## EDUCATION AND THE FRACTURED CONSENSUS

The kind of socioeconomic evolution described in the first part of this chapter, is probably unstoppable in a free society. The statistical evidence makes it clear that human capital is the main economic output of the education system, just as occupational placement is its main sociological function. We may, therefore, propose that the socioeconomy of education needs to be focused on the "human capital order" which defines the class-structure in societies like ours. What the ideological distortions of education do, however, is radically modify and interrupt this key function of the system. If it were not for the influence of the socialist intelligentsia, the middle classes would by now be even larger than they have become. The traditional proletariat would be more shrunken still. As Digby Anderson has pointed out, the socialist intellectuals have even managed effectively to proletarianize the teaching force itself.[28]

In trying, via the education service, to impose socialism on all people, the frantic intellectuals have proletarianized a large section of the population in perpetuity. This is surely quite unacceptable.

None of this is to deny that education works quite well for many people and excellently for some. There is no doubt that education is a source of social control. It is beyond dispute that social ascent for many millions of people has been through education. It is the huge tail of educational underachievement which so appalls us. Would we countenance, in 1995, 30 percent or more of our citizens in terrible housing? Any institution in which people of impressionable age are required to spend a minimum of 15,000 hours is bound to play some part in the social formation of their consciousness. The question is: what sort of consciousness are we speaking of? Given that education is bound up with the job-structure and the network of qualifications typical of a modern economy, the "market-code" of capitalism must be present. It is impossible in a society where the division of labor is so overwhelming a preoccupation, for its imperatives to be excluded from the schools. They are bound to be there. What is at issue is how strongly. What needs ascertaining is the balance of intellectual and ideological influences as these touch different children in different schools and institutions and at different stages of their educational experience.

How far is education an adequate agency of functional consensus, in terms of preparing citizens for active participation in civil society and for the reality of life in a competitive market economy? I hold both that education is inadequate for these crucial purposes and that the specific arrangements of teacher-education are the main reasons that this is so. Basil Bernstein once spoke of education as an "interrupter system."[29] What is interrupted is the reproduction of capitalist society, and teacher-education is one of the main interrupters. The experience of the person passing through the education-system is fractured, various and contradictory. Rival views as to what is important and true will assail different people at different times. The messages of the curriculum bring into the consciousness of its detainees and educands, both the consensus of national tradition, capitalist economy and respect for the civil order of society and the voracious traditions of antinomianism, multiculturalism and anticaptalism typical of the modern socialist movement. We should pity the young people that they must tolerate these radical ambiguities and confusions.

People sometimes make the wrong choices. If we had listened to Durkheim we would not have made such a mess of the schools. It has been left to Durkheim's more cautious and sober modern heirs like Brian Davies, to point out that the education system may not function very effectively, under the weight of the contradictory demands which it must shoulder.[30]

Today, we must surely go much further than Davies did a decade and a half ago. Education transmits dissensus and conflict as well as consensus; it is at times destructive rather than cohesive; it possesses potential for chaos and disorder as well as harmony and control. Education, so far from being the passive or even reactive agency for capitalist reproduction that the neo-Marxists have long insisted, is a proactive engine of socialist ideology. Education epitomizes the ambience of the modern intelligentsia who occupy its most prestigious and lucrative positions. They want the affluence, the restaurants, houses, cars and consumer durables which the modern capitalist economy so effortlessly produces. At the same time, they do all they can to promote socialist ideology and preoccupations.

Education is conceivably the main conduit for the antimeritocratic outlook of the British public, which wants capitalism but would continue to constrain it with envious, progressive taxation. If conservative governments want a less compromised capitalism, they should endeavor to excise some of the socialist ideological clutter from the classroom. The forces of the market have carried the main field but there are campaigns which they have yet to win. Schools are places of schizophrenic coding. The messages of capitalism and the division of labor do come through but in a notably reduced form. At the same time, the endless egalitarianizing of the curriculum missionaries, driven by the inspectors, advisors and teacher-educators, sets up unbearable discords in the public consciousness.

It is important that we do not run away with the idea that education in countries like Japan and Germany is necessarily efficient. I doubt that this is the case. Nor do I think that there was ever a time when British education was efficient. I would not expect any publicly funded activity anywhere to be really efficient. It is a question of degrees of inefficiency. What we have in the British case is the inherent inefficiency of the public sector, compounded by ideologies which militate against the educability of many people. In Japan, by contrast, the assumption seems to be that everyone should be pushed as far as possible.[31] Thus, while the continuous monitoring that a market would give is absent—the system is not economically optima—the distorting and depressive egalitarian ideology is also mercifully absent.

## CONCLUSION

Space does not permit my dwelling on the new alleged horrors of capitalist stratification, those of race, gender and culture. Suffice it to say that insofar as these shortcomings are real, they are absorbable in the secular tendency of markets to radical impersonality, functional indifference to the ascriptive aspects of economic agents. It were better to supply people with human capital than burdensome grievances. A general theoretical statement is now possible. The class-structure of advanced capitalism is given by two main factors, the one major and the other minor. The major element is human capital formation. The minor is the irritating socialist ideological residue of Rousseau and Marx.

# NOTES

1. There is a vast literature on these lines. For an American example, very influential in British sociology in the 1970s and early 1980s, see Bowles, S. and Gintis, H. *Schooling in Capitalist America*, Routledge and Kegan Paul, 1976.
2. Rostow, W.W. *How It All Began*, Methuen, 1975.
3. Potter, J. "Industrial America" in Allen, H.C. and Hill, C.P., *British Essays in American History*, Arnold, 1957.
4. Parsons, T. *Evolutionary and Comparative Perspectives*, Prentice Hall, 1966.
5. Ibid., For a critical commentary see Andreski, S. *Social Sciences as Sorcery*, Andre Deutsch, 1972.
6. Marx, K. and Engels, F., *The German Ideology* (multiple editions); Bourdieu, P. and Passeron, J.C., *Reproduction in Education, Society and Culture*; Marcuse, H., Wolff, P. and Moore, B. Jr., *A Critique of Pure Tolerance*, Cape, 1969.
7. Hayek, F., *The Fatal Conceit*, Routledge, 1988.
8. Bernstein, B.B., *Class, Codes and Control*, Routledge and Kegan Paul, 1977, vol. 3.
9. Blaug, M., *An Introduction to the Economics of Education*, Allen Lane, 1970.
10. Wiles, P.J.D., *Economic Institutions Compared*, Blackwell, 1977.
11. The socioeconomy of status needs further research. It is apparent, however, that when people decide to invest resources in pursuit of particular careers, they often include a weighing of status outcomes on the benefit side of the calculus. People decide to study law, for example, not just for the high income which can result, but for the prestige which such an occupation also generates.
12. Weber, M., *Economy and Society*, Bedminster, 1968, 2 vols.
13. Only in conversation, Seldon (formerly of the Institute of Economic Affairs) is actually sympathetic to the project of an antisocialist sociology.
14. Bowles and Gintis op.cit. In fact, there is a truly vast literature. In recent times, at least, ordinary, workaday

people have often seemed much wiser than "intellectuals." Today, this distinction is clearly exemplified in the way intellectuals cling to various socialist ideas whem most people have abandoned them.

15. Kolakowski, L., *Main Currents of Marxism*, Clarendon, 1978, 3 vols.

16. Wittfogel, K.A., *Oriental Despotism*, Yale University, 1963.

17. Voslensky, M., *Nomenklatura*, Bodley Head, 1980.

18. Flew, A., *Thinking about Social Thinking*, Harper Collins, 1991.

19. Crosland, A., *The Future of Socialism*, Cape, 1981.

20. Halsey, A.H., et al., *Origins and Destinations*, Clarendon, 1980; Goldthorpe, J.H., *Social Mobility and Class-Structure in Modern Britain*, Clarendon, 1980.

21. O'Keeffe, D.J., *Progress and Atonement: A Critique of Multi-Culturalism in Education*, Campaign For Real Education, 1992.

22. The government has introduced a number of improvements. There is more information about schools and examination results and so on available to citizens now. But compared to the information available as to consumer durables, etc., our routine knowledge of education-data remains thin.

23. Adult Literacy and Basic Skills Unit, *Literacy, Numeracy and Adults*, 1987.

24. O'Keeffe, D.J., *The Wayward Elite*, Adam Smith Institute, 1990.

25. Levy, D., *Realism*, Carcanet, 1981.

26. Schumpeter, J.A., *Capitalism, Socialism and Democracy*, Unwin, 1987.

27. Marsland, D., *Seeds of Bankruptcy*, Claridge, 1988.

28. Anderson, D., *The Sunday Telegraph*, August 6, 1989.

29. Bernstein, op.cit.

30. Davies, B., *Social Control and Education*, Methuen,m 1975.

31. Lynn, R., *Educational Achievement in Japan*, Social Affairs Unit, 1988.

# CHAPTER 10

# THE FUTURE OF WORK AND WORK RELATIONS

*Alfredo Tamborlini*

I shall treat the topic I have been assigned from the particular viewpoint of the Institute of which I am director: Isfol (Istituto per lo sviluppo della formazione professionale dei lavoratori), which in Italy is the governmental research institute on the problems of labor, employment, orientation, trades, new technologies and training. Isfol focuses on action-research, experimentation and technical assistance vis-a-vis its institutional partners to develop innovative models. The results of its research are presented in the Annual Report to the Ministry of Labor.

The production, spread and effective utilization of new technological resources in the course of the history of industry must be set in the context of the birth, progressive growth and decline of certain "paradigms of development" endowed not only with technical but economic, organizational and cultural dimensions that are interconnected in internally cohesive models.

Thus, technological innovation forges ahead primarily because it responds to certain problems—economic ones, above all—which a given society encounters and for which the previous paradigm no longer provides satisfactory responses. Entering into the social relations, institutional structures and overall culture of that same society, it then contributes to the recasting of society. This process of remodeling begins with the sphere that is fundamental to every social reality—the organization of production—and drives the educational, juridical and political institutions to adjust to the new technical and economic demands until a new paradigm of development has been fashioned.

On the basis of this conceptual outlook, international research in the past several years has shed light on the obsolescence of the paradigm of mass industry which, introduced by Ford at the start of the century, sustained and guided postwar economic development.

In the 1980s, the spreading wave of technological innovations, based on microelectronics and information processing, has sought to respond to the structural rigidity of the system of mass production. The new technologies (NTs) permit a swifter and more effective adjustment to the evolution of the market and to the growing demands for a "customization" of products, in accordance with the dictates of the emerging paradigm of "flexible specialization."

In parallel, the model of organization of labor also is changing; here, too, firms are pursuing objectives of enhanced flexibility that include, from the temporal stand-point, the request that labor be performed on the basis of schedules and procedures more closely fitted to the productive needs of the moment.

To this trend we must add the tendency arising from the growing demand for flexibility from individuals and the quest for optimal combinations between one's professional life and one's off-the-job interests. Today, this demand encounters fewer impediments in the organization of production and, in certain respects, it may even be seconded by technological innovation. We have only to think of telework; of the new magnetic badge clock-in, clock-out systems that simplify the introduction of flexible work schedules; of the overall shift of employment toward the services sector, making atypical work schedules more common; and of the growth of office work or indirect work at the expense of labor directly engaged in production, and the attendant tendential decline in the proportion of workers whose time is directly tied to the operational demands of machinery.

Technological innovation seems to favor a loosening of the rigidities of the temporal organization of labor for another reason as well: the accelerating rate of change requires permanent updating of the human factor and makes not only more practicable but more necessary, the various initiatives or proposals that have been made for alternation between training and work, in a prospect of permanent education.

A second issue of considerable interest in connection with the relationship between NTs and working life concerns the procedures for implementing technological and organizational innovation in the sphere of employed labor.

Two aspects, in particular, merit closer examination: first, subjective evaluation of the effects of technological innovation on the various dimensions of the quality of work; second, judgment of the procedures followed in introducing the changes, especially in regard to the participation and training of the workers involved.

To begin with, it must be remarked that the debate on technological change in productive processes and on the transformation of work has, in recent years, struck a more optimistic note than had been prevalent in the 1970s. In that decade, there was a wide audience for a pessimistic reading of technological innovation, which was held responsible for a sharp impoverishment of the contents of work and was viewed as the source of a tendential polarization between a narrow hyper-skilled top level and a mass of de-skilled operatives, reduced to merely carrying out fragmented, routine tasks.

In the 1980s, instead, the decline of the "Fordist" paradigm of mass industry has generated the search for new models for organizing production and new technological solutions to the problems of turbulent markets and heightened international competition.

The computer-based NTs are characterized by high flexibility of application and, therefore, by a marked non-determinism of modes of implementation; in other words, the NTs do not impose an organizational model of their own, and very different models of organization can be linked to the very same type of technology. Nonetheless, what is most prevalent today in the debate on the evolution of productive systems is the idea of "flexible specialization," or of the "flexible firm," as the new technical and organizational paradigm.

In contrast with the traditional Fordist model, this approach asserts that technological innovation entails increased skill, training and responsibility for blue-collar workers; a tendential transition from rigidly delimited tasks to broader and more versatile occupational roles; a lesser degree of separation between the moment of *conception* and the moment of *execution*; an effort to tap the workers' experience and insights by means of forms of productive organization that are conducive to cooperation instead of conflict.

The tendency, therefore, would be to go from a fundamentally "low- trust" system of labor relations to a "high-trust" system pivoting on mutual confidence and collaboration between managers and managed.

At the same time, however, it can be observed that corporate management seems to have introduced the process of innovation substantially through top- down procedures, that is, with little involvement on the part of the individuals concerned, or their representatives. While several forms of participation have been implemented, they have been routed through a relationship with the trade unions only to a marginal extent; more frequent are the cases of forms of direct participation at the request of management, especially at the white-collar level.

Thus, what seems to emerge is a substantially traditional approach to the introduction of NTs in the workplace, based still on a clearcut separation between conception of the innovative process and purely executive roles.

Apparently, the discussion in recent years on the use of human resources, on the importance of acknowledging the know-how accumulated on the job, on the need to elicit this know-how in new forms of dialogue between managers and managed, on the necessity that the workers cooperate actively if innovation is to succeed, has yet to find widespread application in practice. Nonetheless, the insights that gave rise to this "participationist" current in the debate on the organization of labor seem to have found confirmation, among part of the workers, in an awareness that they possess an unacknowledged fund of experience and suggestions for a more effective introduction of the NTs.

Both technological innovation and organizational innovation appear to be occurring in "diffusive" and "de-specializing" forms, that is, they are realized through the concourse of a plurality of corporate functions and departments, thanks to a generally high elasticity of corporate structures and an equally high general adaptability to change on the part of the personnel.

On the plane of business organization, the most notable trend is the steady emergence of the business-network as an organizational model capable of responding to many of the needs of innovation. Even when they do not resort to forms typical of the business-network, to govern their interactions, firms are constantly creating organizational instruments that are a departure from pure marketplace relationships. Decision-making processes, therefore, tend to be multilateral, and strategic objectives are determined on the basis of evaluations not limited to a single firm. By now, inter-company agreements stand as an alternative to expansion and higher investment within the confines of an individual firm.

Technological innovation, the essential engine of development of productive processes, products and office work, is generally accompanied by an intense marketing effort. In the sphere of their marketing strategies, we may note the tendency of firms to: 1) concentrate on a single field; and 2) effect "mass customization" of their products, that is, to build differentiated products from standardized basic components, in order to satisfy the needs even of limited segments of the market.

Firms show a marked propensity to organizational transformation. "Hybrid" structures are arising that are not cast along the lines of "pure" organizational models (by function, by division, and so forth) but are compounded of elements characteristic of different forms. The functional model is still the most widespread, but the emerging tendencies are well represented by *transitional structures* in which both functional and divisional elements are present.

This tendency has to be seen in the light of the need of firms to manage the complexity of their environment and strategies through multifunctional capacities that allow corporate cultures and individual outlooks and insights to converge on a multiplicity of objectives.

For the structures—and for the persons working in them—the updating of know-how becomes more and more crucial. Activities are directed not only to functional concerns (e.g., to raise production, to reduce costs) but to many-sided problems (e.g., to innovate a product line) that require intense interaction among different components of the organization, a high degree of operational flexibility and constant recourse to delegation of authority.

The organization's cohesiveness must, therefore, be ensured by a series of *mechanisms of integration* such as:

a. "ad hoc meetings" of managers on specific problems, characterized by a high degree of "personalization" of relationships;

b. recourse to *formal roles of integration and coordinations* (e.g., product manager, project manager) and dedicated structures (task-forces that cut across the corporate structure horizontally and obliquely, helping different units converge on common objectives);

c. utilization of *operational planning and control systems* which, providing managers at least monthly feedback on follow-up to decisions, represent the organization's real "central nervous system."

Nevertheless, the key to integration and organizational coordination is constituted by *personnel policies* clearly oriented toward the values of flexibility. Compared to companies in the other industrial countries, Italian firms have developed formalized techniques of personnel management to a lesser extent. This should be interpreted as a deliberate strategic orientation geared, for example, to shift individuals rapidly in accordance with the performances of business, to plug in outside resources when necessary, to open up new career paths swiftly, and so forth. The most highly developed managerial instruments, thus, are the ones that concern *selection* and *training,* while techniques of evaluation, incentives and career-path definition find relatively limited application. In other terms, Italian firms utilize mainly those instruments which permit them to have at their disposal professional resources that are actually able to deal with high levels of complexity and uncertainty, to the detriment of instruments keyed more closely to the regularity of job performance.

In general, personnel policies have been marked by a partial but significant recovery of employment; the demand for labor has reacted positively to the expansive trends.

The innovative trends may be said to entail a substantial reformulation of the training strategies most closely linked to them and a rethinking of the pertinent "teaching methodologies." In the future, the new strategies will have to be fitted, not so much to the "contents of training," as to the *overall requirements for knowledge, information and know-how* that are emerging in the different contexts of innovation.

From this standpoint, it will probably also be necessary to rethink many traditional elements connected with the place of training in terms of social evaluation, investment and operative structures. The proximity of training to the *education function* remains evident, but there is an increasingly close relationship between training and the *Research and Development function*, typically dedicated to the growth of the intangible resources of greatest important in the innovative processes. A very considerable portion of training still consists of "direct" activity (the classroom), but a growing proportion—and one which prevails from the qualitative standpoint—consists of indirect or integrated activity in "meta-training" interventions whose aim is organizational innovation.

The development of the new phase of training ought, therefore, to be accompanied by a renewed interest in the principles underlying the training function and by a number of practical choices such as: to foster this development in the most critical areas.

The foregoing overview of the most recent forms taken by technological innovation suggests that it would be appropriate to underscore the new horizons that are opening up in the relationships between training and technology.

In the light of the most important studies and research in this field, it can be said that new synergies and new multiplier effects are arising between approaches to training and advanced technological processes.

These synergies are essentially the expression of far-reaching changes that have arisen in the culture of training. In particular, phenomena, tendencies, theoretical conceptions, methodological options, strategies and active policies are being fashioned and are appearing in the field of training whose common denominator is their growing attention for and interpenetration with the processes of innovation based on science and technology.

Owing to its quantitative and qualitative dimensions and its wide-ranging implications, the importance of the theme of the connections between training and technology is tangibly reflected in the development and spread of what may safely be called an emerging area of training research and specialization: the area of "technological training," which regards the study of advanced training processes in the field of the new technologies, both as a direct object of knowledge and as an instrument for accessing, conveying and diffusing knowledge.

Schematizing, we may identify this new context's salient elements as follows:

a.  development of the training function conceived as the chief vehicle or, more exactly, as the primary source of socialization of innovation for the productive organizations which have promoted the training initiative and/or to which it is ultimately addressed;

b.  a new prevalence of teaching and training methodologies and techniques with respect to the specificity of contents;

c.  evolution of the contents of training away from strictly high-tech and narrowly applicable formulae toward contents providing high value-added and a greater deferred return on the invested capital (both financial and human);

d.  broadening of the logical, technical and geographical horizons and scenarios in which the new transactions in the training market are framed, with particular reference to the prospect of European integration;

e.  growth of increasingly complex and high-structured forms of collaboration and consortia (thanks also to the formation of integrated information networks and systems) among those who promote, materially realize and are the final beneficiaries of training;

f. sharper focus on the part of these new training models and opportunities on young people graduating from (or still enrolled in) specialized courses of study (university level or the equivalent).

As appears evident, the above-listed elements composing the innovative framework are closely interconnected and thus can be observed as a whole.

Furthermore, the approaches underlying them can be observed and summarized by two parallel interpretations.

The first interpretive key concerns the growing transnational dimension that the productive sectors and the connected occupational and training systems are assuming under the pressure of technological innovation. In particular, the current processes of innovation at the productive and occupational level are shaping common characteristics and tendencies, but also common problems and requirements, for an ever greater number of contexts and areas which, though geographically "distant" or belonging to different countries, are logically homogeneous and "near" in terms of models of development and innovative processes.

The point is that a process is underway marked by the broadening out, merging and complex internal development of the traditional fields and specialized technological disciplines into large "technological sectors" such as biotechnologies, communication technologies, processing and automation technologies, and so forth.

Already plugged into (or hoping to plug into) these technological macro-sectors endowed with a high strategic and propulsive value are productive and occupational contexts that, while logically homogeneous, are distributed over the European panorama in a very uneven and fragmented fashion.

The same innovative processes are making areas or contexts that are geographically close or belong to the same nation more distant and remote from each other, in terms of rates and models of development, potentialities and capacities to accumulate resources.

The results of the recent studies promoted by the European Economic Community (EEC) on the new socioeconomic geography of Europe are extremely indicative in this sense. The new configuration consists of some six European scenarios, each composed of a homogeneous group of regions (scattered geographically and belonging to different nations), as identified by a set of indices of socioeconomic development (or underdevelopment). What emerges is a Europe proceeding with "many speeds" and with markedly different faces, which makes it imperative to undertake new, more effective strategies to integrate the development processes. This holds particularly true for Italy, since the EEC survey shows that Italy is represented, with differentiated areas and their attendant models of development, in nearly all six levels of the European panorama—from the most propulsive to the most marginal and critical.

Concerning the implications of all this on the level of training systems, there is a more and more widely perceived need to redesign and refashion the occupational resources required for the governance and diffusion of increasingly advanced productive systems in accordance with parameters and approaches that are receptive to the new scenarios opened up by innovation: new homogeneities or "logical contiguities" between economic and productive contexts and/or occupational systems in regard to "technological sectoralities" which do not take into account spatial and geographical distance or proximity or national identity.

It follows that the skills, know-how and career paths of the emerging occupational figures have to be planned and built by means of a substantial broadening of the cultural frames of reference and nationally-based qualifications of those to be trained (and, implicitly, of the trainers as well). This must be done, in particular, in line with criteria of integration, interchange and connection between training sources and models capable of offering the keys of access to a transnational occupational and employment market.

Furthermore, the growing complexity and specialization of knowledge and the rapid obsolescence of occupational skills make it more and more necessary to develop training processes based on a combinatorial, modular, skill- transferable logic. What is needed, in other words, is an approach such as to permit rapid, specialized and qualitatively high-level updating, retraining and extended training programs; that is, programs that to an increasing degree prove relevant and transferable to ever-widening spheres of science and technology, production and skills.

By the same token (and indeed even more so), for the occupational and skill areas that are more backward—or, for whatever reason, are less caught up in the processes of innovation—and for the supply of labor (young people, especially), that is still in a marginal position, the horizons of training processes have to be broadened so as to amplify the opportunities of integration with more advanced contexts and areas. This must be done through specific training and mobility plans tapping appropriate aggregates and sources of skills from which crucial resources can be drawn and transferred.

An additional interpretive key lies in the promotional impetus supplied by the new Community strategies that have been implemented in support of the more general objective of forging the single internal market by the end of 1992. The Community strategies have, no doubt, created new, wider horizons for innovation in educational policies and strategies. In particular, a more concrete European dimension has opened up in which to frame the development of advanced training processes in the field of the new technologies. In this dimension, the latter play a decisive role, both as a strategic object of knowledge and as an instrument of access to knowledge.

# THE FUTURE OF WORK AND WORK RELATIONS

In accordance with the movement underway toward the creation of the European single market, the EEC is promoting and supporting programs in favor of the European economic and occupational identity presently being formed. We may cite, in particular, the series of initiatives for advanced technological training (continuing and basic) that have been jointly elaborated and implemented by representatives of production and training at the national level, but whose theoretical and operational points of reference are the European context and the available specific Community programs of support.

These initiatives substantially concern the development of emerging occupational skills incorporating advanced science and technology. They seek to accomplish this by means of a methodologically innovative training process based on the mobility and transnational transferability of the contents and objectives of training, of the trainees, and of the training products or supports that are created.

The political options and strategic visions underlying these initiatives are of great cultural importance and carry enormous weight for the evolution of the role to be assumed by training processes in the European identity presently being formed.

In the first place, it is an initial assumption that the construction of a real European identity can be accomplished only by constructing active linkages connecting the economic and productive structures, the dynamics of the market and the European occupational systems. In other words, the process of technological, productive and occupational development already underway for some time in the various European contexts is emphatically reaffirmed to be a priority vehicle or strategic carrier of real European unification. And, in fact, this process has already produced, and is increasingly producing, an "upward homologation" of an economic, social and cultural nature on the European plane that is far more active and concrete than anything achieved on the strictly political and institutional level.

A further significant option underlying this proliferation of Community programs in support of the technologies/training/integrated European development nexus can be glimpsed in the growing importance and significance attributed to training policies. The latter are substantially viewed as a "transmission belt" of European socioeconomic development, that is, as a structured and permanent system of resources devoted to linking, fueling and adjusting the processes which, as is indicated above, are considered the greatest "guarantors" of the European identity and European development.

The integrated development of the two aforementioned phenomena—the innovative processes on the technological, productive and occupational level, on the one hand, and the active EEC policies of European integration on the other—is steadily persuading the protagonists of training processes to project their training policies and the attendant investments in a transnational dimension, that is, in a very much broader technological, economic and cultural frame of reference.

The conviction is widely held by now that it is improper to interpret the trends and characteristics of employment by isolating the technological variable alone in the sphere of the complex phenomenon of innovation.

An analysis of the demand for occupational skills emerging from innovative contexts underscores that it is the connection between strategic, organizational and technological innovations that reveals the possibility of a different utilization of the human factor. The same connection points to occupational figures which are new even in respect to a recent past, and are diversified in accordance with the needs peculiar to the various realities of production. An analysis of the demand for occupational skills also points up the stratification of the internal labor markets and a relative growth of their importance in the context of personnel management policies. The stratification of the internal labor markets is a function of decisions made in the course of processes of delegation, by which term we mean human delegation, effected in attributing autonomy and responsibility, and technological, manual or intellectual delegation.

The relative growth of the importance of occupational skills to personnel management policies can be attributed to a series of factors that are both external to companies, that is, they are related to the trends in the labor market, and are internal to them.

Both phenomena can be better understood if closer examination is given to the relationship between processes of innovation and the role of the human factor, and if this viewpoint (which is also that of residuality in respect of technology's potentialities and limits and of the consequent processes of delegation) is adopted in interpreting the equally complex problem of the demand for training.

The hypothesis taken as a point of departure in analyzing this problem identifies the lessening of the devastating impact of the recent leap from the technological paradigm of the past as the opportunity for a less anxiety-ridden study of the discontinuity which that leap has produced in the processes whereby the skills required from the human factor are defined.

*According to this hypothesis, what training must contend with today is not so much a problem of reconversion and adjustment as it is the necessity of redefining its own contents and methodologies at various levels.*

The relationship between processes of innovation, demand for occupational skills and the problems of training has been analyzed in a series of research studies that Isfol has made of cases of technological and organizational innovation.

It is appropriate to clarify that the decision to start with an analysis of contexts that are experimenting with innovation—a choice that diverges from the fruitful strand of research that correlates the strategies of utilization and management of human resources with the organizational models adopted—does not derive from any judgment regarding the "excellence" of the solutions being tried out. Nor does it stem from any hypothesis regarding the immediate exportability of these solutions to other contexts. On the contrary, starting from an analysis of realities in which innovation is seen not only as a cultural paradigm but as a practical realization, the intent is to stress that the complex nature of the processes currently underway gives rise to multifold, specific organizational decisions, spiking any hypothesis of determinism and indeed emphasizing the significant nature of those decisions.

The contexts in which the decisions in question are made represent a fertile field of study. In these contexts, the demand for new occupational models takes on special urgency and appears widespread in various areas and at various organizational levels; it is true, however, that rarely does this urgency find expression in a definite design, a meticulous specification of needs or a well-defined planning of training.

In contexts characterized by the introduction of appreciable innovations, we can note how the technological given points to more complex processes in which the different types of innovation can also proceed in parallel.

For non-manual workers in particular, strategic and organizational innovations are what have the greatest impact on the emergence of new occupational models.

It is possible, in fact, to note a narrowing of the distance between the strategic moment and the operational moment, and a diffusion to various organizational levels of the activities whereby strategic orientations are defined and realized. Thus, there is a diffusion of an objective-focused culture, which often gives rise concretely to project-centered forms of organization, to task forces, and to a concentration on the in-house promotion of entrepreneurial forms and activities.

In several cases, one can note a tendency to arrange the process of strategy definition in such a way as to involve different points and levels of the organization, and the widespread inclination to center the structure of the organization of labor and the overall plan of skill distribution on the attribution of clearly defined objectives. Organizational systems, pressed to control exceedingly volatile markets, thus are tending more and more toward organicity, seeking subjective solutions to the common need of flexibility.

For firms that produce goods, the search for flexibility essentially is expressed through plant automation and the computerization of information and planning systems.

In these cases, flexibility means not only the capacity to convert to different product lines at limited cost, but also the capacity to be versatile, working on several products simultaneously, and to be elastic, modifying output volumes in a short span of time.

For firms operating in the services sector, flexibility answers the need to be able to provide the most customized services possible and to track customers closely, using computerized information systems in order to identify promptly any new market segments.

In both situations, we can also note an emerging demand for flexibility being made by individuals. This demand is framed in terms of versatility and elasticity; as yet, it would be hard to translate it into terms of individual skills.

An analysis of the research findings on non-manual workers suggests a two-pronged approach to this problem. On the one hand, we find a blurring of the confines separating several categories of professional roles, such as the technician, the manager, the entrepreneur, the researcher, and the consequent oblique spread of several skills and responsibilities (akin to what is taking place in manual labor for the tasks of regulating, control, maintenance and testing). On the other hand, we can note the request for a methodological approach to the carrying out of various types of activities based on the relationship between elements that are clearly defined (instruments and objectives) and procedures that are not rigidly prescribed.

The defining of new professional figures today, hinges precisely on the question of how to carry out an activity, which is the focus of the newest and relatively most neglected part of the planning of training.

To reach their objectives, organizations whose concern with the attribution of objectives is growing apace with the potentiality of their technological endowment have to pursue paths that entail utilization of technical skills (the instrumental base) but that also involve managerial and relational skills, skills in decoding signals (not just the symbols proper to the field of technology but organizational and economic symbols as well), skills in heeding the relationship between constraints, resources and opportunities, skills in creative analysis and solution of problems.

Thus, at various levels there is a diffusion of skills that previously fell in the domain of specific professional roles, and there is a tendency to make the methodologies of work uniform.

A spreading need to know how more things are done can, like the concept of labor flexibility, harbor the risk of breeding a generic request for multivalence or cause excessive vagueness in the defining of occupational spheres or lead to a constant under-utilization of skills. Research has sought to surmount this obstacle by hypothesizing and testing for the existence of a type of skill that can be defined as basic, in that it is designed to prepare the individual as a worker (irrespective of the occupational role he or she fills) who acts in contexts destined to undergo more and more rapid change. In view of the changing nature of jobs and of the labor requested of the human factor, this sort of basic training for work cannot be acquired, once and for all, as a core on which to build the evolution of skills, but instead must be of a recurring nature.

# THE FUTURE OF WORK AND WORK RELATIONS

The task of this sort of training will be to lay the foundation in terms of disciplinary, cross-disciplinary and methodological skills that can be engaged in the realization of various roles and in different organizational contexts. It constitutes a central element of professionalism. And, in addition to being articulated in specific contents, it also impinges on the structure and interrelations of the traditional basic disciplines, with which it cannot be made to fit perfectly, and especially on the method by which they are transmitted.

The foregoing diagnosis of the demand for professionalism permits the formulation of hypotheses concerning the contents of basic training for work also in relationship to the educational system (since it is a body of skills that should find a legitimate place in the school system and in primary and secondary-level vocational training). It also permits hypotheses to be framed in regard to the paths and even the scheduling of access to training. As was stated above, basic training for work does not entail contents targeted solely to young people. A series of implications follow from this observation. On the one hand, it raises questions of a marked methodological nature concerning the fashioning of an effective approach to adult education. On the other, it poses a problem of defining the scheduling and places best suited to this type of training activity, suggesting the hypothesis of routes that are no longer linear (school, work, exit from the labor market) but are circular, in which periods of work alternate with periods of training in the life of an individual.

This hypothesis raises yet another problem, bearing on the issue of training sites and on the relationship between the national training system and company training programs. As an hypothesis, we might envisage the transition from a model, based on current tendencies, in which the national training system follows criteria of inclusion (of disciplines and contents) and in-house training in the company follows criteria of exclusion (except when it is forced to make up for the failings of the educational system), to a model whereby the national training system would be selective and complementary to company training programs. Under this hypothesis, by providing basic training for work, the school system and vocational training system would fulfill a real task of constructing and, through recurrent training, altering the structure of occupations, while a company-level training would shoulder the task of adapting this basic training to the realities of specific contexts (sectors, departments, areas), to particular organizational approaches, and to the carrying out of specific roles in the company.

This reading of the relationship between the emerging organizational models and the problems of training validates the hypothesis that training should be viewed as a social investment and resource for development, and that it is central not only to social policies, but to labor policies as well.

# NOTES ON CONTRIBUTORS

**DAVID MARSLAND** is Professor of Social Sciences and Director of the Centre for Evaluation Research at the West London Institute of Higher Education (UK). He is the winner of the first Thatcher Award, presented in 1991 by Margaret Thatcher for contributions on the analysis of freedom. He has published extensively on social theory and social policy. His books include *Seeds of Bankruptcy: Sociological Bias Against Business and Freedom* (Claridge Press, 1988), and (with Ralph Segalman) *Cradle to Grave: Comparative Perspectives on the State of Welfare* (Macmillan, 1989).

**JOHN CHODES** is a historian and libertarian writer in New York City (USA), and the author of numerous studies of the history of freedom. His recent publications include *Public Education and Indoctrination* and *Education for a Conquered Nation*.

**ADRIAN FURNHAM** is Professor of Psychology at University College (University of London, UK). He is the author of fifteen books and some 300 scholarly papers. His recent publications include (with B. Stacey) *Young People's Understanding of Society* (Routledge, 1990).

**ALFRED HIMELSON** is Professor of Sociology (Emeritus) at California State University at Northridge (USA). He has researched and published extensively in the fields of employment and criminology.

**DENNIS O'KEEFFE** is Professor of Sociology and Director of the Truancy Unit at the University of North London (UK). His recent books include *The Wayward Elite: A Critique of British Teacher Education* (Adam Smith Institute, 1990), and *Truancy in English Secondary Schools* (Department of Education, 1993).

# WORK AND EMPLOYMENT

**W.T. (THEO) ROY** is Professor of Politics Emeritus at the University of Waikato, New Zealand. He has researched and published widely in the fields of history and politics.

**PETER SAUNDERS** is Professor of Sociology at the University of Sussex (UK). His several books include *Social Class and Stratification* (1990), *A Nation of Home Owners* (1990), and *Privatisation and Popular Capitalism* (1994).

**RALPH SEGALMAN** is Professor of Sociology (Emeritus) at California State University in Northridge (USA). He is author of many books and papers including *Dynamics of Social Behavior and Development* (University Press of America, 1979), *Poverty in America* (with A. Basu, Greenwood, 1981), and *The Swiss Way of Welfare* (Praeger, 1986).

**ALFREDO TAMBORLINI** is Director of the Institute for the Development of Professional Training (ISFOL) in Rome, Italy. He has researched extensively on developments in the technology and organization of work.

**WALTER E. WILLIAMS** is John M. Olin Distinguished Professor of Economics at George Mason University (Virginia, USA). He is author of many well-known books, including *South Africa's War Against Capitalism*.